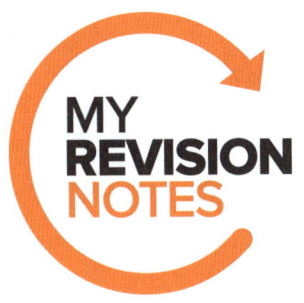

My Revision Notes

Cambridge National

Level 1/Level 2

HEALTH AND SOCIAL CARE

SECOND EDITION

For the J835 specification

Judith Adams

The Publishers would like to thank the following for permission to reproduce copyright material.

Photo credits

p13 © Civil / Shutterstock; p14 © create jobs 51 / Shutterstock; p17 t © Jacob Lund - stock.adobe.com, b © SeventyFour Images / Alamy Stock Photo; p18 © Cathy Yeulet / 123RF; p20 © ALPA PROD/Shutterstock.com; p25 © Igor Zakowski / Shutterstock; p39 © michaeljung/stock.adobe.com; p40 © Dean Mitchell/deanm1974/Fotolia.com; p42 © Monkey Business/stock.adobe.com; p43 © Barry Barnes / 123RF; p45 © Monkey Business/stock.adobe.com; p51 © DGLimages / Shutterstock; p53 © Monkey Business/stock.adobe.com; p55 © SBphotos/stock.adobe.com; p56 © Phanie / Alamy Stock Photo; p57 © Andrey Popov / stock.adobe.com; p60 © Crown Copyright; p61 © Rawpixel.com/stock.adobe.com; p62 © amazing studio/stock.adobe.com; p63 © Monkey Business/stock.adobe.com; p65 © R. Gino Santa Maria/stock.adobe.com; p70 t © John Birdsall / Alamy Stock Photo b © kitamin/123RF.com; p71 © Dean Mitchell/iStock / Getty Images; p73 © NPCC; p75 l-r © BSI Group, © The British Toy & Hobby Association, © European Commission The Lion Mark was developed by the British Toy and Hobby Association (BTHA) which supply around 90 per cent of toys sold in the UK. It was developed in 1988 to act as a recognisable consumer symbol denoting safety and quality.

Every effort has been made to trace all copyright holders, but if any have been inadvertently overlooked, the Publishers will be pleased to make the necessary arrangements at the first opportunity.

Although every effort has been made to ensure that website addresses are correct at time of going to press, Hodder Education cannot be held responsible for the content of any website mentioned in this book. It is sometimes possible to find a relocated web page by typing in the address of the home page for a website in the URL window of your browser.

Hachette UK's policy is to use papers that are natural, renewable and recyclable products and made from wood grown in well-managed forests and other controlled sources. The logging and manufacturing processes are expected to conform to the environmental regulations of the country of origin.

Orders: please contact Hachette UK Distribution, Hely Hutchinson Centre, Milton Road, Didcot, Oxfordshire, OX11 7HH. Telephone: +44 (0)1235 827827. Email education@hachette.co.uk Lines are open from 9 a.m. to 5 p.m., Monday to Friday. You can also order through our website: www.hoddereducation.co.uk

ISBN: 978 1 3983 5124 0

© Judith Adams 2022

First published in 2022 by Hodder Education (a trading division of
Hodder & Stoughton Limited),
An Hachette UK Company
Carmelite House
50 Victoria Embankment
London EC4Y 0DZ

www.hoddereducation.co.uk

The authorised representative in the EEA is Hachette Ireland, 8 Castlecourt Centre, Dublin 15, D15 XTP3, Ireland (email: info@hbgi.ie)

Impression number   10 9 8 7 6

Year   2026 2025

All rights reserved. Apart from any use permitted under UK copyright law, no part of this publication may be reproduced or transmitted in any form or by any means, electronic or mechanical, including photocopying and recording, or held within any information storage and retrieval system, without permission in writing from the publisher or under licence from the Copyright Licensing Agency Limited. Further details of such licences (for reprographic reproduction) may be obtained from the Copyright Licensing Agency Limited, www.cla.co.uk

Cover photo

Typeset in India

Printed and Bound in Great Britain by Bell & Bain Ltd, Glasgow

A catalogue record for this title is available from the British Library.

Get the most from this book

This book will help you to revise for your Cambridge National in Health and Social Care exam (Unit R032: Principles of care in health and social care settings). You can find out more about the exam on page 6.

Everyone has to decide their own revision strategy, but it is essential to review your work, learn it and test your understanding. These Revision Notes will help you to do that in a planned way, topic by topic. Use this book as the cornerstone of your revision and don't hesitate to write in it: personalise your notes and check your progress by ticking off each section as you revise.

Tick to track your progress

Use the revision planner on page 4 to plan your revision, topic by topic. Tick each box when you have:
- revised and understood a topic
- tested yourself
- practised exam questions.

You can also keep track of your revision by ticking off each topic heading in the book. You may find it helpful to add your own notes as you work through each topic.

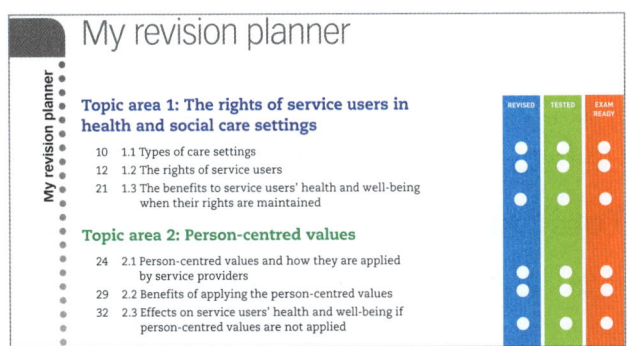

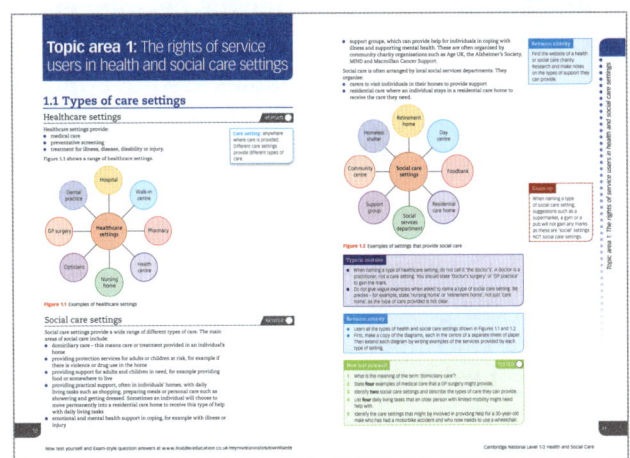

Features to help you succeed

Exam tips

Expert tips to help you polish your exam technique and maximise your chances in the exam.

Typical mistakes

Common mistakes made by other students and guidance on how to avoid them.

Now test yourself

Short questions to test your knowledge and understanding as you work through the course. Answers can be found at the back of this book.

Revision activities

Revision activities to guide your note-taking.

Definitions and key words

Clear, concise definitions of essential-to-know terms.

Exam-style questions

Practice exam questions. Use them to consolidate your revision and practise your exam skills. Answers are given online at **hoddereducation.co.uk/myrevisionnotesdownloads**

Cambridge National Level 1/2 Health and Social Care

My revision planner

Topic area 1: The rights of service users in health and social care settings

- 10 1.1 Types of care settings
- 12 1.2 The rights of service users
- 21 1.3 The benefits to service users' health and well-being when their rights are maintained

Topic area 2: Person-centred values

- 24 2.1 Person-centred values and how they are applied by service providers
- 29 2.2 Benefits of applying the person-centred values
- 32 2.3 Effects on service users' health and well-being if person-centred values are not applied

Topic area 3: Effective communication in health and social care settings

- 36 3.1 The importance of verbal communication skills in health and social care settings
- 38 3.2 The importance of non-verbal communication skills in health and social care settings
- 40 3.3 The importance of active listening skills in health and social care settings
- 42 3.4 The importance of special methods of communication in health and social care settings
- 45 3.5 The importance of effective communication in health and social care settings

Topic area 4: Protecting service users and service providers in health and social care settings

- 49 4.1 Safeguarding
- 56 4.2 Infection prevention
- 64 4.3 Safety procedures and measures
- 77 4.4 How security measures protect service users and staff

80 Now test yourself answers

94 Glossary

95 Index

Answers to Exam-style questions online at www.hoddereducation.co.uk/myrevisionnotesdownloads

Countdown to my exams

From September

- Attend class in person or via the internet if necessary; listen and enjoy the subject; make notes. Make friends in class and discuss the topics with them.
- Watch the news.

REVISED

6–8 weeks to go

- Start by looking at the specification – make sure you know exactly what material you need to revise and the style of the examination. Use the revision planner on page 4 to familiarise yourself with the topics.
- Organise your notes, making sure you have covered everything on the specification. The revision planner will help you to group your notes into topics.
- Work out a realistic revision plan that will allow you time for relaxation. Set aside days and times for all the subjects that you need to study and stick to your timetable.
- Set yourself sensible targets. Break your revision down into focused sessions of around 40 minutes, divided by breaks. These Revision Notes organise the basic facts into short, memorable sections to make revising easier.

REVISED

2–6 weeks to go

- Read through the relevant sections of this book and refer to the exam tips, exam summaries, typical mistakes and key terms. Tick off the topics as you feel confident about them. Highlight those topics you find difficult and look at them again in detail.
- Test your understanding of each topic by working through the 'Now test yourself' questions in the book. Look up the answers online.
- Make a note of any problem areas as you revise and ask your teacher to go over these in class.
- Look at past papers. They are one of the best ways to revise and practise your exam skills. Write or prepare planned answers to the exam practice questions provided in this book and check your answers online.
- Use the revision activities to try out different revision methods. For example, you can make notes using mind maps, spider diagrams or flash cards.
- Track your progress using the revision planner and give yourself a reward when you have achieved your target.

REVISED

One week to go

- Try to fit in at least one more timed practice of an entire past paper and seek feedback from your teacher, comparing your work closely with the mark scheme.
- Check the revision planner to make sure you haven't missed out any topics. Brush up on any areas of difficulty by talking them over with a friend or getting help from your teacher.
- Attend any revision classes put on by your teacher. Remember, they are an expert at preparing people for examinations.

REVISED

The day before the examination

- Flick through these Revision Notes for useful reminders, for example the exam tips, exam summaries, typical mistakes and key terms.
- IMPORTANT: Check the time (is it morning or afternoon?) and place of your examination. Keep in touch with other students in your class.
- Make sure you have everything you need for the exam – pens, highlighters and water.
- Allow some time to relax and have an early night to ensure you are fresh and alert.

REVISED

My exams

Unit R032 Paper

Date: ....

Time: ....

Location: ....

Cambridge National Level 1/2 Health and Social Care

Introduction to Unit R032 Principles of care in health and social care settings

Exam breakdown

The written exam

You will complete a written examination:
- Unit R032 Principles of care in health and social care settings.

The exam is set and marked by the OCR examination board. The examination paper is worth 70 marks.

In the examination you will be tested on four topic areas:
- Topic area 1: The rights of service users in health and social care settings
- Topic area 2: Person-centred values
- Topic area 3: Effective communication skills in health and social care settings
- Topic area 4: Protecting service users and service providers in health and social care settings.

Questions might be about a particular topic area or might require answers that combine information from two or more different topic areas.

How long will I have to complete the exam?

The examination lasts for 1 hour and 15 minutes.

Unit R032 covers three performance objectives (POs):
- PO1 Recall knowledge and show understanding
- PO2 Apply knowledge and understanding
- PO3 Analyse and evaluate knowledge and understanding.

Structure of the question paper

The examination paper will include:
- a range of short and medium-length questions worth a total of 50 marks
- one extended response question worth 8 marks – this will assess performance objective 3 (PO3); responses will need to include discussion or evaluation
- two extended response questions worth 6 marks each.

What type of questions will appear in the exam paper?

You can expect to find a wide range of question types on the paper, for example:
- some 1-mark questions requiring a one-word answer
- multiple-choice questions
- short-answer questions worth 2 to 4 marks
- longer extended response questions worth 6 to 8 marks.

Exam-style question answers at www.hoddereducation.co.uk/myrevisionnotesdownloads

None of the individual parts of a question will be worth more than 8 marks.

You must answer all of the questions.

Context-based questions

Some questions will be context-based. This means that the questions are based on care setting scenarios. You have to apply your knowledge to produce a response that is relevant to the care setting scenario.

Example settings could include a GP surgery, a nursing home, a day centre, a hospital, a shelter for the homeless, a retirement home or a homeless shelter.

You will need to apply your knowledge of the R032 topics to produce an answer that is relevant to the scenario you are given.

Fact- and knowledge-based questions

Some questions will be fact- and knowledge-based. These questions will not be based on any particular care setting.

Preparing for the exam

- Find the specimen papers and mark schemes on the OCR website. Have a go at a paper and mark it yourself using the mark scheme.
- Always ask your teacher if you don't understand something or are not sure – your teacher is there to help you.
- It is never too early to start revising. Begin your revision by going through your handouts and notes after each lesson – don't just file them away!
- Remember, the more times you go through a topic, the more you will remember.
- Make a revision plan a timetable with dates. Use the revision planner at the front of this book to tick off each topic you have revised.
- Use the revision activities suggested in this book so that you don't get bored just reading through notes all the time.
- Learn the key terms for each topic so that you are able to correctly use specialist terminology in your answers.

Exam command words

All of the questions will have a 'command word' – this will tell you what you have to do to answer the question.

Examples of command words, starting with the easiest to the more demanding, are shown below.

Command word	Meaning
Circle	• Select an answer by circling one of the options given
Choose	• Select an answer from the options given
Annotate	• Add information, for example to a table or diagram
Identify	• Select an answer from options given • Recognise, name or provide factors or features • Give brief information or facts such as naming, stating or listing
Fill in, label or complete	• Add information, for example to complete a table, diagram, chart or graph
State	• Give factors or features • Give short, factual answers
Outline	• Give a short account, summary or description • Give the key aspects or facts about something
Describe	• Give an account including all the relevant characteristics, qualities or events • Give an account of all the relevant facts, features, qualities or aspects of something
Explain	• Give more depth and detail than a description. You will include relevant reasons for, causes of, purposes of or effects of something • Use words or phrases such as 'because', 'therefore' or 'this means that'
Justify	• Give good reasons for offering an opinion or reaching a conclusion
Analyse	• Separate information into components and examine it methodically and in detail in order to explain and interpret it • Explain the pros and cons of a topic or argument and make reasoned comments • Explain the impacts of actions using a logical chain of reasoning
Discuss	• Give an account that considers a range of ideas and viewpoints • Present, analyse and evaluate relevant points (for example, for/against an argument)
Assess	• Give a reasoned judgement or opinion of the quality, standard or effectiveness of something, informed by relevant facts
Evaluate	• Make a judgement about something by taking into account different factors and including strengths and weaknesses or positives and negatives • Make a reasoned qualitative judgement considering different factors and using available knowledge/experience

Always check the command verb carefully before answering a question. If you describe something when an explanation is required, you will not be able to gain full marks – this is because an explanation requires more detail than a description.

Exam-style question answers at www.hoddereducation.co.uk/myrevisionnotesdownloads

Exam technique – top tips!

There is more to producing a good answer to an exam question than simply knowing the facts. The quality of your response, such as how you organise your answer and whether it is fully relevant to the question, will help you gain extra marks.

- Read each question carefully at least twice before you start your answer.
- Underline or highlight the command word so that you are clear about what you have to do.
- If a question asks for 'ways' without saying how many ways, you must give a minimum of two as 'ways' is plural. The same applies to 'methods', 'reasons', etc.
- For higher-mark questions (6 to 8 marks), write your answer in paragraphs. Each paragraph should focus on a specific aspect of the answer. This ensures your answer is organised and logical.
- Make sure the information in your answer is accurate and relevant to the question. Don't just write everything you know about a topic – answer the question!
- Be guided by the number of marks and space provided for the length of your answer. The more marks, the more space will be provided. Unless you have very large handwriting you should not need to continue your answer on to the extra pages at the end of the examination paper.
- If you do continue your answers on the extra pages, make sure you state the question number and the part of the question, for example 3(b) or 6(a), so that the examiner marking your paper knows exactly which question you are answering.
- Do not leave any questions unanswered even if you feel you don't know the answer. Have a go – you probably know more than you think you do!

Topic area 1: The rights of service users in health and social care settings

1.1 Types of care settings

Healthcare settings

REVISED

Healthcare settings provide:
- medical care
- preventative screening
- treatment for illness, disease, disability or injury.

Figure 1.1 shows a range of healthcare settings.

> **Care setting** Anywhere where care is provided. Different care settings provide different types of care.

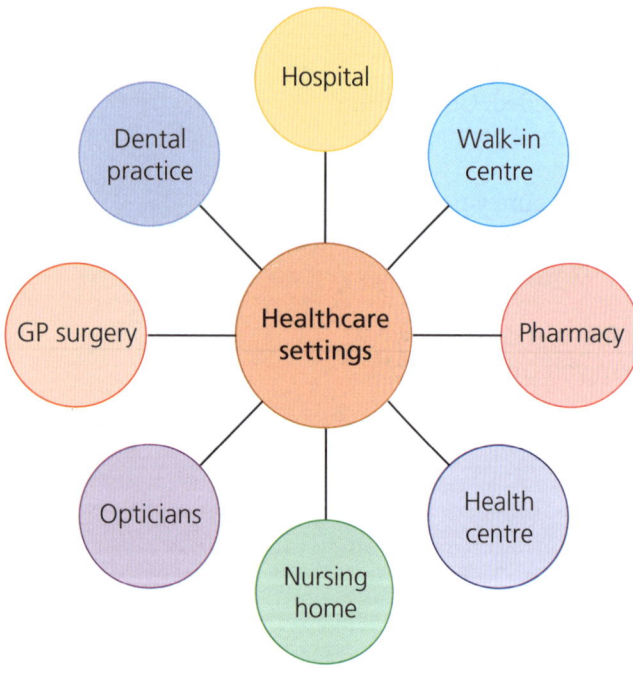

Figure 1.1 Examples of healthcare settings

Social care settings

REVISED

Social care settings provide a wide range of different types of care. The main areas of social care include:
- domiciliary care – this means care or treatment provided in an individual's home
- providing protection services for adults or children at risk, for example if there is violence or drug use in the home
- providing support for adults and children in need, for example providing food or somewhere to live
- providing practical support, often in individuals' homes, with daily living tasks such as shopping, preparing meals or personal care such as showering and getting dressed. Sometimes an individual will choose to move permanently into a residential care home to receive this type of help with daily living tasks
- emotional and mental health support in coping, for example with illness or injury

Exam-style question answers at www.hoddereducation.co.uk/myrevisionnotesdownloads

- support groups, which can provide help for individuals in coping with illness and supporting mental health. These are often organised by community charity organisations such as Age UK, the Alzheimer's Society, MIND and Macmillan Cancer Support.

Social care is often arranged by local social services departments. They organise:
- carers to visit individuals in their homes to provide support
- residential care where an individual stays in a residential care home to receive the care they need.

> **Revision activity**
>
> Find the website of a health or social care charity. Research and make notes on the types of support they can provide.

Figure 1.2 Examples of settings that provide social care

> **Exam tip**
>
> When naming a type of social care setting, suggestions such as a supermarket, a gym or a pub will not gain any marks as these are 'social' settings NOT social *care* settings.

> **Typical mistake**
>
> - When naming a type of healthcare setting, do not call it 'the doctor's'. A doctor is a practitioner, not a care setting. You should state 'doctor's surgery' or 'GP practice' to gain the mark.
> - Do not give vague examples when asked to name a type of social care setting. Be precise – for example, state 'nursing home' or 'retirement home', not just 'care home', as the type of care provided is not clear.

> **Revision activity**
>
> - Learn all the types of health and social care settings shown in Figures 1.1 and 1.2.
> - First, make a copy of the diagrams, each in the centre of a separate sheet of paper. Then extend each diagram by writing examples of the services provided by each type of setting.

> **Now test yourself** TESTED
>
> 1 What is the meaning of the term 'domiciliary care'?
> 2 State **four** examples of medical care that a GP surgery might provide.
> 3 Identify **two** social care settings and describe the types of care they can provide.
> 4 List **four** daily living tasks that an older person with limited mobility might need help with.
> 5 Identify the care settings that might be involved in providing help for a 30-year-old male who has had a motorbike accident and who now needs to use a wheelchair.

1.2 The rights of service users

The rights of individuals

REVISED

- Everyone is entitled to rights.
- Rights are set out by laws such as the Equality Act.
- Service providers and practitioners who support individuals' rights will be working within the law and providing a high standard of personalised care.

Figure 1.3 shows the rights that all individuals are entitled to.

Laws Passed by Parliament and state the rights and entitlements of service users. If someone breaks the law, they can be prosecuted by being taken to court.

Equality Act A law which aims to ensure service users are treated fairly.

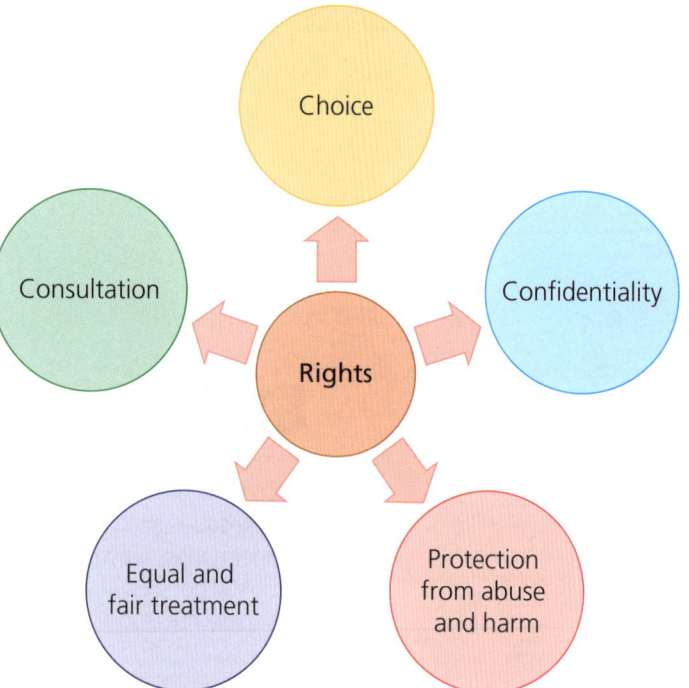

Figure 1.3 Individual rights of service users

Exam tip

Learn the five rights. Make sure you can name them all correctly.

Revision activity

To help you remember the rights, use a mnemonic: three 'Cs and a 'PE'.
- Choice
- Confidentiality
- Consultation
- Protection from abuse and harm
- Equal and fair treatment

Now test yourself

TESTED

1. Write a list of **four** groups of individuals that are entitled to rights.
2. Are rights set out by policies or by law?
3. List the **five** rights to which individuals are entitled.

Exam-style question answers at www.hoddereducation.co.uk/myrevisionnotesdownloads

Choice

REVISED

Having choices:
- gives individuals control over their lives
- promotes independence
- empowers individuals
- increases self-esteem
- makes individuals feel valued.

> **Self-esteem** How much a person values themselves and the life they live.

Choice in residential social care settings

Examples of providing choice in residential social care settings include:
- offering a range of activities for residents to take part in
- giving residents a choice whether or not to take part in activities
- supplying a range of menu options such as vegetarian, gluten free, Halal, Kosher
- residents deciding which clothes to wear today
- residents choosing what time to get up and to go to bed
- ensuring residents choose whether they have a bath or a shower
- providing both a TV lounge and a quiet room
- providing an optional programme of social events and outings.

Figure 1.4 A variety of meal choices should be available in care settings

> **Exam tip**
>
> Often exam questions will be set in the context of a specific care setting. Make sure your answer refers to that particular type of care setting. For example, if you are asked for examples of how care practitioners could provide choice for residents in a retirement home, do not give answers that relate to a hospital because this would limit the marks you could achieve.

Choice in residential healthcare settings

Examples of providing choice in healthcare settings include providing choice over:
- where to receive care – support at home or in a residential setting
- which GP to see
- consultation with a male or female doctor
- hospital food options that take account of special dietary needs
- whether or not to receive treatment
- the type of treatment they want to receive
- how they receive help and support.

> **Vegetarian** A diet in which no meat or fish is eaten.
>
> **Gluten free** A diet that does not include the grains wheat, barley and rye, which can trigger a dietary intolerance in some individuals.
>
> **Halal** A diet in which no pork is eaten and all meat has to be prepared according to Muslim law.
>
> **Kosher** In Judaism, this is used to describe something that is 'correct' – food that is sold, cooked or eaten satisfying the requirements of Jewish law. Meat and dairy cannot be eaten at the same meal.

> **Typical mistake**
>
> - Don't give vague or unrealistic examples of choice, such as 'letting them do whatever they like' for young adults in a day centre.
> - Make sure you can name the rights accurately. Don't get them muddled up, for example by stating 'equal choices' or 'fair choices'.

> **Revision activity**
>
> Create a set of revision cards for different types of care settings, giving examples of choices that should be available in each setting – for example, a hospital, a day centre and a hostel for homeless adults.

> **Now test yourself** TESTED
>
> 1. Write a definition of the term 'choice'.
> 2. Identify **two** different ways in which a young adult resident of a nursing home could be given choice.
> 3. Identify **two** different ways nursing staff on a hospital ward could support a patient's right to choice.
> 4. How could a GP surgery provide choice for its service users?

Topic area 1: The rights of service users in health and social care settings

Cambridge National Level 1/2 Health and Social Care

Confidentiality

Care workers and practitioners have access to a lot of personal information about the individuals they are caring for. This information should only ever be shared on a need-to-know basis.

The rights of individuals to have their information protected are set out in a law named the General Data Protection Regulation (GDPR). Confidentiality limits access to, or places restrictions on, sharing certain types of information so that it is kept private.

Why is confidentiality so important?

Confidentiality is important because:
- care workers often receive very sensitive and private information from service users
- service users may be vulnerable and very trusting of those caring for them
- it is unprofessional to talk about confidential matters outside of the care environment
- it protects the interests of any individual
- it helps service users to trust their carers
- the service user's permission must be obtained before information is passed on to people outside the care team.

> **Need-to-know basis**
> Information is shared only with those directly involved with the care and support of an individual.
>
> **Confidentiality** Limits access to or places restrictions on sharing certain types of sensitive information so that it is kept private and can only be accessed by those who need to be aware of it.

Figure 1.5 Service users' personal information should be shared on a need-to-know basis only

Need-to-know basis

- Information is shared only with those directly involved in the care and support of an individual.
- Access to the information is restricted to those who have a clear reason to access it when providing care and support for an individual.
- Sharing information means telling a practitioner the facts they need to be aware of, at the time they need to know them, in order to provide care for the individual, and nothing more.
- If something is said on a need-to-know basis, a practitioner can only tell it to the relevant people. For example, if a teacher was concerned about a child's welfare, they would tell the head of year, not all the other teachers in the school.
- Care workers should always inform service users that they cannot keep all information secret and that sometimes it has to be shared with others involved in the individual's care.
- In certain, very specific circumstances, confidentiality has to be broken. Details of these circumstances are shown in Table 1.1 on the next page.

> **Exam tip**
>
> Make sure that you understand the term 'need-to-know basis' and that you can give an example of it in practice.

Exam-style question answers at www.hoddereducation.co.uk/myrevisionnotesdownloads

Table 1.1 Times when confidentiality has to be broken

When the individual:	Examples
intends to harm themselves	• Person says they are going to commit suicide • Mental health problems where they threaten to, or do, harm themselves
intends to harm others	• Threatens to seriously injure someone • Mental health problems where behaviour puts others at risk of harm
is at risk of harm from others	• Suspected child sex abuse • A case of domestic violence
is at risk of carrying out a serious offence	Such as: • terrorism • drug dealing

> **Revision activity**
>
> Copy out Table 1.1. Cut up the table to separate the circumstances and the examples. Mix them all up. Correctly match the examples with the circumstances.

Ways of maintaining confidentiality in health and social care settings

- Do not gossip about the service users with their friends and family.
- Share information with other practitioners only on a need-to-know basis – and only with those directly involved in caring for the individual.
- Keep patient records secure: lock them in a filing cabinet or, if stored electronically, keep them password-protected.
- Keep personal details, files and records safe and secure by not leaving them lying around the care setting for unauthorised people to see.
- Use a private office or empty room for meetings with residents or their family to discuss treatment or care.
- Do not discuss patients, residents or other service users in public places.
- Inform service users of circumstances when information cannot be kept confidential – for example, because the service user is a danger to themselves or to others, or is at risk of harm.

> **Typical mistake**
>
> It is a mistake to state that confidentiality means keeping everything 'secret'. Remember, care workers are not allowed to 'keep secrets'. All information relevant to the care of an individual has to be shared with all of the team caring for that person.

> **Now test yourself** TESTED
>
> 1 Write a definition of 'confidentiality'.
> 2 Give an example of how a social worker might share information on a need-to-know basis.
> 3 Give **two** examples of circumstances when confidentiality has to be broken.
> 4 Explain why confidentiality is important in care settings.

Consultation

REVISED

It is important that individuals are consulted and involved in the decision-making process for their own care and support. This requires service users to work in partnership with the practitioners providing their care and the relevant support services.

Consultation could take place directly with the service user themselves or through a service user's representative, such as a family member, friend or advocate.

> **Consultation** The process of discussing something with someone in order to get their advice or opinion, so that a decision can be made that is acceptable to all involved.
>
> **Advocate** Someone who speaks on behalf of an individual who is unable to speak up for themselves.

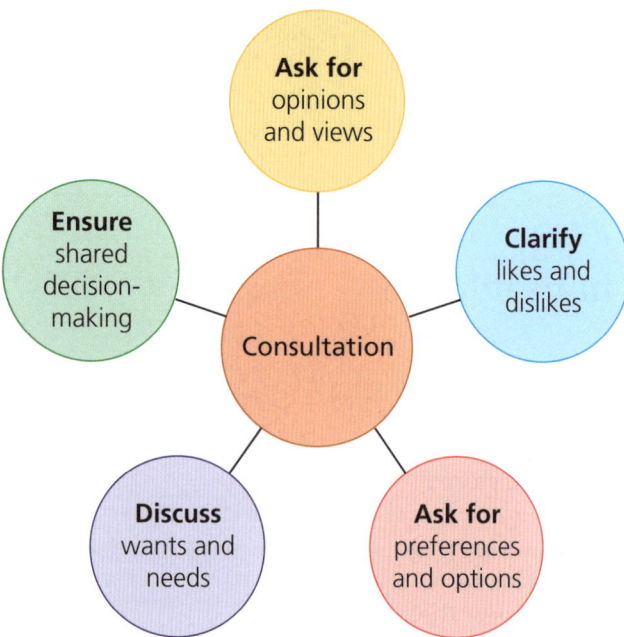

Figure 1.6 Aspects of consultation

Ways practitioners can support an individual's right to consultation

- Ask for their opinion.
- Listen to their views.
- Ask what type of care they would like, if it were possible.
- Give information about the options available to them.
- Provide information about different treatments and explain their benefits and disadvantages.
- Explain what different treatment options will involve.
- Share decision-making based on the individual's opinions.

> **Typical mistake**
>
> Make sure you do not mix up the rights of 'choice' and 'consultation' – be sure you know the difference. Remember that choice means to select from options you have been given, while consultation means discussing and exploring possible options.

How consultation supports rights

Consultation means seeking the individual's views and opinions so their personal preferences can be taken into account, informing their choice of care provision.

This means individuals feel:
- valued and listened to
- in control
- empowered to make an informed choice
- confident that the care meets their individual needs.

Exam-style question answers at www.hoddereducation.co.uk/myrevisionnotesdownloads

Figure 1.7 Getting to know an individual

> **Revision activity**
>
> Figure 1.7 shows a care worker having a discussion with a retirement home resident. Make a list of questions that the care worker could ask to support the resident's right to consultation.

> **Now test yourself** — TESTED
>
> 1. Write a definition of 'consultation'.
> 2. List **four** features of consultation.
> 3. Identify **two** ways in which a social care practitioner could support an individual's right to consultation.
> 4. Explain how a hospital doctor could support a patient's right to consultation regarding their treatment.

> **Exam tip**
>
> Make sure you can give examples of consultation for practitioners in both healthcare and social care settings. Exam questions are often based on a particular setting, such as a GP surgery or a residential care home.

Equal and fair treatment

REVISED

Equal treatment means being given the same opportunities and choices as everyone else.

Fair treatment means being able to have full access to those opportunities and choices, as well as receiving the type of care that meets individual needs.

Figure 1.8 Considering the accessibility needs of people with disabilities, for example by installing a wheelchair ramp, is one way of making products, services and facilities accessible to everyone.

Example 1

Staff at a day centre for young adults have arranged to take them to a theatre workshop. Some of the young adults have hearing impairments. The day centre staff have arranged for all of the activities to be signed (with British Sign Language). This will enable all the young adults to fully take part and enjoy the day.

Example 2

It is important that children with *special educational needs* can take part in the same lessons as the rest of their class. This ensures equality of opportunity. Without extra support, children with special educational needs might struggle with the classwork, which would not be fair treatment.

School children with special educational needs can be enabled to stay with their class if they are given extra support, for example differentiated worksheets (these have instructions for different abilities, for example) and tasks. This might also include one-to-one support from a teaching assistant who could, for example, help them understand the work, act as a translator or use sign language.

In this way, being treated differently ensures the children have equal opportunities.

Individuals using health and social care and early years services should be treated fairly and:
- in accordance with the Equality Act (a law that supports equality and fair treatment)
- in such a way that their individual needs are met, as shown by the two examples above.

Why equal and fair treatment?

Equal and fair treatment means individuals are:
- given the same opportunities and choices
- enabled to have the same access as others to opportunities and choices
- treated according to their individual needs.

Remember, treating people fairly means treating them in the way most appropriate to their individual needs. This may mean care workers treat some individuals differently than others because different people have different needs. For example, a teaching assistant may give a child help with maths on a one-to-one basis while the rest of the class is taught as a group. The child having one-to-one help is being given special treatment and support to enable them to catch up and develop the same level of skills as the rest of the class.

> **Special educational needs** Learning or physical disabilities, for example hearing or visual impairments, or conditions such as ADHD or autism.

Figure 1.9 A teaching assistant providing extra support in the classroom

> **Revision activity**
>
> For health and social care services try to think of three examples, for each, where individuals are treated differently in order to ensure they have equal opportunities.

Typical mistake

It is a mistake to state that 'treating everyone the same' is equal treatment. People have to be treated in line with their individual needs. Remember: different individuals have different needs and so need to be treated differently.

Now test yourself — TESTED

1. Explain the difference between 'equal treatment' and 'fair treatment'.
2. Explain how a college that provides wheelchair ramps is supporting individuals' rights.
3. Why is 'that they are an individual' the most important piece of information a care worker should remember about the person they are caring for?

> **Exam tip**
>
> Learn the definitions of 'equal' and 'fair' treatment. Be able to explain the difference.

Protection from abuse and harm

All care settings need to follow safeguarding procedures to protect children and adults. The Care Quality Commission (CQC) gives the following definition of safeguarding:

'Safeguarding means protecting people's health, wellbeing and human rights, and enabling them to live free from harm, abuse and neglect. It's fundamental to high-quality health and social care.'
(Source: www.cqc.org.uk/what-we-do/how-we-do-our-job/safeguarding-people)

See also Topic area 4.1, page 49.

Procedures to protect care workers and service users from abuse and harm

All staff must:
- have DBS checks (see Topic area 4.1, page 55)
- follow reporting procedures for abusive behaviour
- attend safeguarding training.

All care settings must:
- appoint a Designated Safeguarding Lead (DSL)
- have clear and up-to-date:
  - complaints procedures
  - fire procedures
  - emergency evacuation procedures
  - lockdown procedures
  - policies on, for example, confidentiality, equal opportunities, 'no secrets'
- provide staff with training in:
  - manual handling
  - safeguarding
  - first aid
- hold regular fire drills (see Topic area 4.3, pages 72–3)
- carry out risk assessments of equipment and activities (see Topic area 4.3, pages 68–9)
- fully implement health and safety law, e.g. Health and Safety at Work Act
- ensure high standards of hygiene in the care setting (see Topic area 4.2, page 56)
- ensure proper security measures are in place (see Topic area 4.4, pages 77–8).

> **Exam tip**
>
> Make sure you can give examples of procedures to protect care workers and service users from abuse and harm in each type of care setting – healthcare and social care.

When are abuse and harm more likely to occur?

Abuse and harm are more likely to occur if staff are not trained properly in:
- how to use equipment, so may injure themselves or those in their care – for example, when transferring someone out of a bath using a hoist
- manual handling, so may injure someone they are caring for or themselves – for example, when moving a service user from a bed to a chair
- correct procedures when providing intimate care, such as bathing, changing continence pads, so may be accused of abuse
- diversity and equality, so incidents involving prejudice and discrimination are more likely to occur
- safeguarding procedures, so are unaware of their role in dealing with suspected abuse or harm.

Safeguarding Measures taken to reduce the risks of danger, harm and abuse.

DBS checks Criminal record checks carried out by the Disclosure and Barring Service to help prevent unsuitable people working in health and social care services.

Manual handling Using the correct procedures when physically moving any load by lifting, putting down, pushing or pulling – for example, transferring a patient from a chair to a bed.

Security measures All the actions taken within a care setting to protect individuals – for example, controlling access and identifying staff and visitors.

Diversity The recognition that everyone is different and has different needs, so appreciating and respecting individual differences such as a person's faith, diet, ethnicity and customs.

Equality Enabling individuals to have the same rights, access and opportunities as everyone else regardless of gender, race, ability, age, sexual orientation or religious belief.

Prejudice A dislike of, or negative attitude towards, an individual, often based on ill-informed personal opinion. Examples include racial prejudice and homophobia.

Discrimination The unjust and unfair treatment of individuals based on their differences, such as race, religious beliefs, disability or gender.

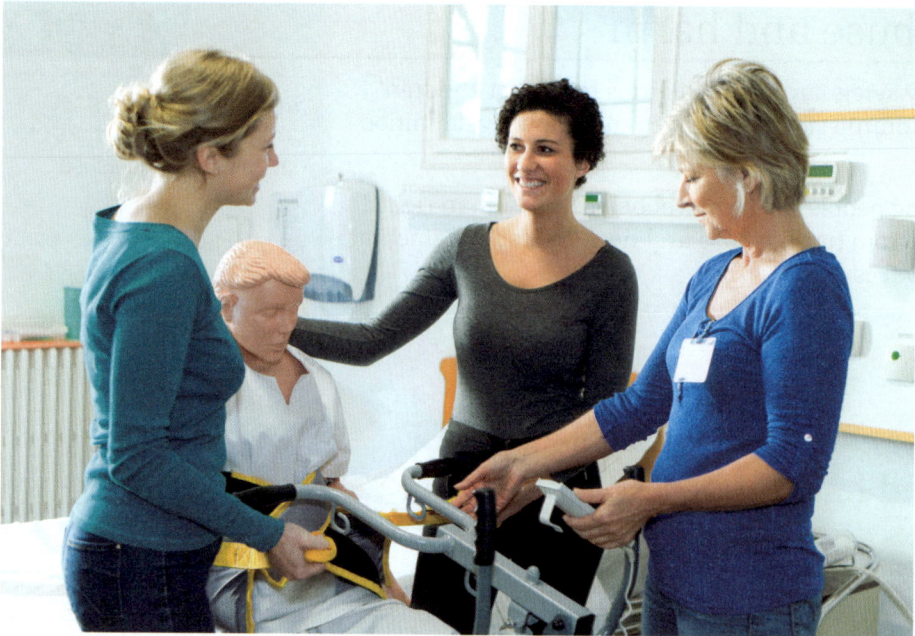

Figure 1.10 Training is essential to avoid injuring service users or care workers when using a hoist

In addition, abuse and harm are more likely to occur if:
- staff are not DBS checked, meaning it is not known whether they have a criminal record and have been barred from working with vulnerable adults and children, so putting the individuals in their care at risk
- there is a shortage of staff, meaning staff are rushed and may neglect service users due to lack of time, or may get impatient, for example if someone with dementia is taking 'too long' to get dressed.

Finally, it is important that staff carry out careful checks of:
- equipment and furniture, such as hoists, chairs, toys, games – if these are old and/or damaged, they could cause injury
- activities and visits – these need to be risk assessed so potential hazards and ways of avoiding them are identified.

Revision activity

Create a concept map for this topic. It should cover the main information relating to:
- procedures to protect care workers and service users from harm and abuse
- individuals who are most at risk from abuse
- when abuse and harm are more likely to occur.

Typical mistake

Do not use the wrong terminology for this topic. In order to gain the highest marks, make sure you know the meaning of terms such as safeguarding, manual handling and discrimination, and use them accurately.

Now test yourself

TESTED

1. Identify **four** procedures that would help to reduce the risk of abuse and harm in a care setting.
2. Identify **three** individuals who may be at greater risk of abuse or harm when in a care setting and give a different reason why for each.
3. What do the initials DBS stand for?
4. How does the DBS ensure that an individual is suitable to work with children or vulnerable adults?

Exam-style question answers at www.hoddereducation.co.uk/myrevisionnotesdownloads

1.3 The benefits to service users' health and well-being when their rights are maintained

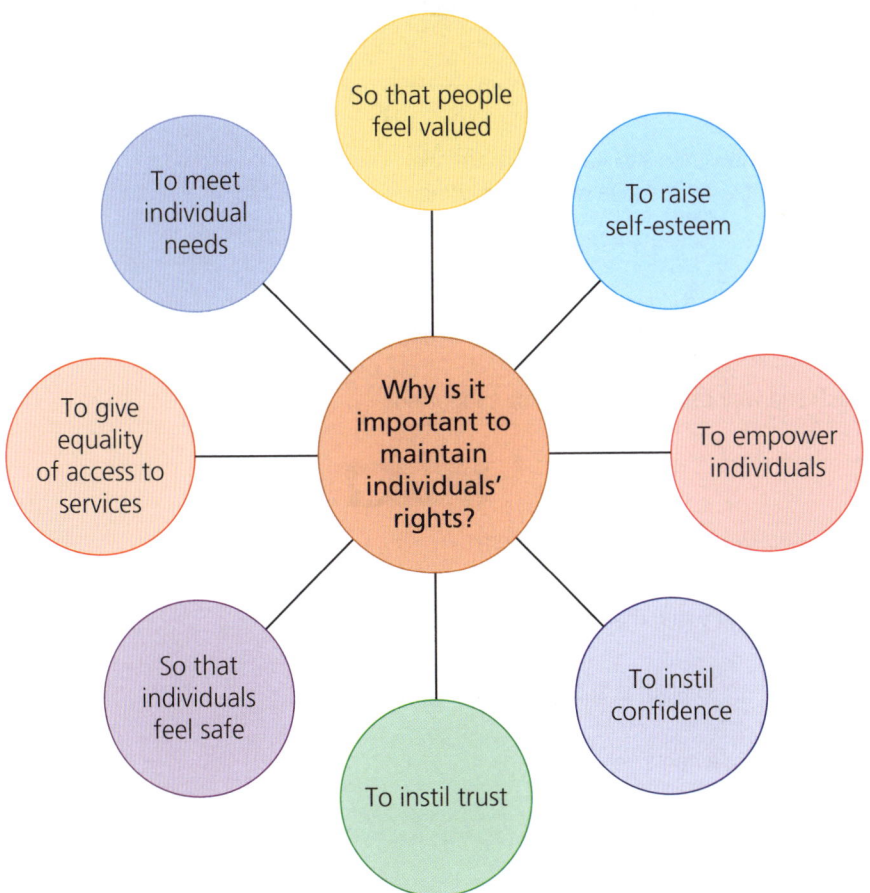

Figure 1.11 Benefits of maintaining individuals' rights

The primary benefits for individuals when their rights are maintained are outlined in Table 1.2.

Table 1.2 Maintaining an individual's rights can have several benefits

Benefit	How this works
Empowerment	• This is to give someone the authority or control to do something. • This is how a health or social care worker encourages an individual to make decisions, take control of their life and become independent.
High self-esteem	• A person with high self-esteem feels valued and respected. • High self-esteem is associated with people who are happy and confident, with positive mental health. • An individual with low self-esteem can experience feelings of unhappiness and worthlessness.

The individual's needs are met	• Receiving appropriate care or treatment supports improvements in mental and physical health.
	• It will help individuals to recover from injury or illness, or learn to manage a disability or health condition, and still enjoy and achieve in life.
	• Care workers will ensure needs are met by, for example:
	  • arranging for mobility aids
	  • meeting dietary requirements
	  • arranging counselling
	  • to ensure physical, emotional and mental health needs are met.

Trust	• Individuals must be able to feel that care workers:
	  • are trustworthy
	  • will not harm them
	  • have the individual's best interests at heart.
	• Individuals who lack trust may not want to continue with the care they should be receiving. This could have negative effects on their physical and mental health and well-being.

Additional benefits of maintaining rights include:

- confidence – individuals will feel that they can rely on care workers and services to get high-quality care that meets their needs
- equality – individuals will be able to access the care they need; adaptations will be made if necessary for them to access care
- safety – care workers and care settings that support individuals' rights to safety will follow health and safety laws and ensure staff are trained in safeguarding procedures.

Revision activity

Create a brief information sheet to be given to a new care assistant at a residential care home. The sheet is a guide to key aspects of good practice when supporting individuals' rights.

Include:
- a specific example of how to support each of an individual's rights (choice, confidentiality, consultation, equal and fair treatment, protection from harm and abuse)
- an explanation of the benefits to health and well-being of rights being supported.

Now test yourself

TESTED

1. In your own words, write definitions of 'empowerment' and 'self-esteem'.
2. List **four** benefits of maintaining an individual's rights.
3. Describe **three** ways in which individuals benefit when their right to make their own decisions about care is supported.
4. Give **three** examples of how an individual's rights could be supported to ensure their needs are met.
5. Describe **two** possible impacts of a lack of trust when a service user is receiving care.

Exam-style question answers at www.hoddereducation.co.uk/myrevisionnotesdownloads

Exam-style questions

1. Identify the type of care setting that would provide the care described in these examples:
   a. Practical support in a service user's own home with daily living tasks such as personal care, for example having a shower and preparing breakfast.
   b. Medical and residential care for older adults. [2]
2. Discuss the difference between care workers providing 'choice' and 'consultation' for their service users.
   Use examples to support your discussion points. [6]
3. Describe **one** way a care worker can ensure confidentiality when using electronic records. [2]
4. Mrs Smith is in hospital. She will be having treatment for her stomach problems. Consultation is one of the rights Mrs Smith is entitled to.
   Explain **three** ways that the doctor looking after Mrs Smith could support her right to consultation. [8]
5. Write a definition of the term 'rights'. [2]
6. The table below lists ways that care settings can support individual rights.

Ways of supporting an individual's rights	Right
Safeguarding procedures in place at a day centre	Protection from abuse and harm
Residents of a care home are provided with a menu of food options at lunchtime	
Ramps and automatic doors are provided at the social services department	
A dentist and a patient have a discussion about treatment preferences	
A social worker sharing information on a need-to-know basis	

For each way, choose the right that is being supported and complete the table. The first one has been done for you. You can use each right once only or not at all.

Rights:
- Choice
- Confidentiality
- Consultation
- Equal and fair treatment
- Protection from abuse and harm
- Trust [4]

7. Read the following extract from High Top Residential Care Home's information booklet. Then answer the following questions.

> High Top Residential Care Home has places for 25 older adults. The manager and staff provide person-centred care which meets the individual needs of all the residents. Residents are asked for their views and opinions regarding decisions about their care. High standards of general hygiene are seen throughout the care home. The gardens are easily accessible by all, with wide pathways and no steps.
>
> When completing our regular satisfaction surveys, residents state that they feel safe and well cared for. They feel safe as the staff are well trained in manual handling, first aid, British Sign Language and there are regular fire drills.
>
> High Top provides a range of activities for residents to take part in, if they wish to, for example crafts, art, gardening and photography. A programme of social gatherings is also available including music, singing, bingo and quizzes. Those who prefer quiet and calmness can make use of the quiet room to relax or for meditation or prayer.

   a. Identify **three** rights of the older adults living at High Top Residential Care Home. [3]
   b. Describe how staff at High Top Residential Care Home are supporting the residents' rights that you identified in part (a) of the question. [8]
8. Describe **one** way a pharmacist could maintain patient confidentiality when discussing test results with a patient at the pharmacy. [2]
9. A GP practice is an example of a healthcare setting. Identify **three** other healthcare settings. [3]
10. List **five** reasons why it is important to maintain individuals' rights in care settings. [5]

Topic area 2: Person-centred values

2.1 Person-centred values and how they are applied by service providers

The person-centred values of care are core principles that underpin the work of those providing health and social care services.

Care workers who apply the person-centred values ensure that individuals using health and social care services receive the most appropriate care. They also help to ensure individuals' needs are met by the care and support services they use.

Person-centred values

REVISED

The person-centred values of care are shown in Figure 2.1.

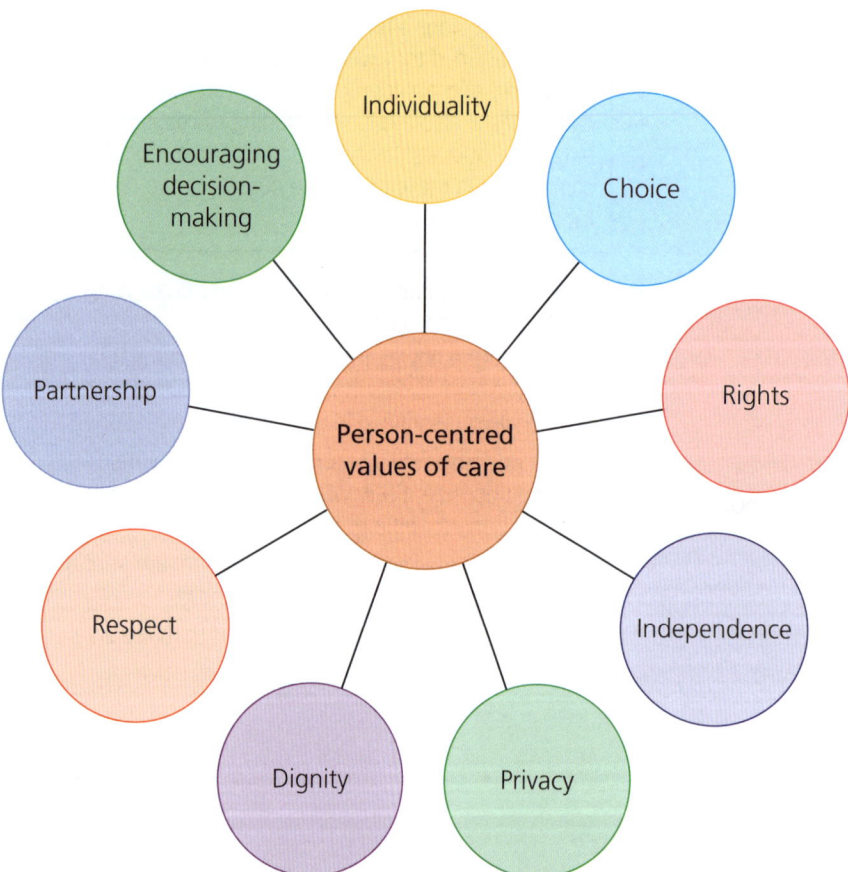

Figure 2.1 The nine person-centred values of care

Person-centred practice is about focusing care on the specific needs of individuals. This ensures that people's needs are met and they can make informed decisions about their care.

Exam-style question answers at www.hoddereducation.co.uk/myrevisionnotesdownloads

Figure 2.2 It is important that service users feel valued and respected by care workers

Some examples of how the person-centred values can be applied by care providers are given in Table 2.1.

> **Inclusion** Involving people in their care to ensure they are treated fairly and are not excluded, for example making care services accessible by providing disability access such as wheelchair ramps or information in Braille or a range of different languages.

Table 2.1 Applying person-centred values of care

Applying person-centred values – what they mean when providing care	

Individuality
Respecting the diversity of individuals working in and using health and social care services
	• The people using, and working in, healthcare and social care services are very diverse, that is they are different and individual.
	• Ways of valuing diversity and promoting **inclusion** in care settings include:
	  • posters and displays that present positive role models from different genders and cultures
	  • respecting individual differences such as faith, language and customs by providing prayer rooms and information in different languages and formats, such as Braille or large print
	  • ramps and lifts to ensure access.
	• Inclusive actions like these help to promote and respect equality and diversity and reduce the risk of discrimination, against any particular group, occurring in care settings.

Choice Enabling individuals to make their own choices	• All individuals are entitled to make their own choices. • Choice is empowering and this is a feature of person-centred care. • Individuals should, for example, be offered a range of care options and given enough information about them to make an informed choice. • Individuals should be able to choose what they want to eat and how they would like to dress.
Rights Helping individuals to understand and access their rights	• Everyone is entitled to rights. • Rights are set out by law. • See Topic area 1.2, page 12 for more information about promoting rights in health and social care.

Applying person-centred values – what they mean when providing care (continued)	
Independence Supporting individuals to be independent	• This involves supporting individuals to be in charge of their life by: 　• providing support to enable them to do as much for themselves as possible 　• keeping them as fully involved in decision-making as possible.
Privacy Allowing individuals to have privacy	• Many procedures in healthcare and social care require privacy, for example showering and dressing, or someone carrying out intimate procedures. • Drawing curtains or closing doors are examples of giving privacy. • It is vital to provide care that respects and protects the individual's privacy. • This also includes not talking about an individual with anyone who is not involved in providing their care.
Dignity Promoting self-respect ensures individuals are never humiliated or embarrassed in any way	• Treating someone well and valuing their opinions and choices promotes a person's self-respect and self-esteem. • When receiving support, individuals still need to feel in control of their lives and treating them with dignity and encouraging decision-making is an important part of this.
Respect The individual's wishes and preferences should be respected	• Respect means taking account of and having regard for someone's feelings, wishes, beliefs and rights. • This means that when you interact with individuals you value their opinions and treat them with dignity and as an individual. • An example would be a social worker listening to and taking account of a client's feelings about not wanting to go and live in a residential care home by finding an alternative, such as providing carers at home.
Partnership Working together with service users and professionals	• This involves different professionals, services and agencies working together to provide the most effective care for an individual requiring treatment or support. • Sharing information and ideas helps people to learn from one another about the ways different people live, think and behave.
Encouraging decision-making of service user	• Service users must always be encouraged to be involved in their care decisions, which should focus on their strengths and abilities. • Care is usually more successful if the individual feels in control of what is happening. • This could be as simple as asking whether they would like a cup of tea or coffee, or what time they need help to get dressed in the morning, rather than doing it for them at a time that suits the carer.

Examples of applying person-centred values of care

- Give service users choice – for example over diet, which clothes to wear, which activities to take part in.
- Maintain privacy – knock on the door before entering a resident's room; pull curtains round a hospital bed.
- Provide access to an advocate for an adult with learning disabilities.
- Provide access to a translator if the service user and care provider do not speak the same language.
- Always explain any procedures to be carried out, as a patient has the right to refuse treatment once they have heard all the necessary information.
- Mobility – ensure all areas and resources are accessible to all by providing, for example, ramps, automatic doors and adjustable-height tables where necessary.
- Provide activities, resources and food that reflect different cultures, beliefs and faiths.
- Celebrate a range of religious and non-religious festivals in the care setting, to reflect the different faiths and cultural needs of the service users.
- Challenge and report any discriminatory behaviour (whether by service users or staff).
- Ensure access to all activities for those less mobile – for example by providing transport and carers to accompany service users on trips, or by visiting wheelchair-accessible venues.

Exam-style question answers at www.hoddereducation.co.uk/myrevisionnotesdownloads

- Respect service users' dietary, cultural and religious requirements; for example:
  - at times it may be appropriate to have a female care assistant, nurse or GP
  - provide prayer rooms and transport to a place of worship, for example a synagogue/church/mosque
  - provide appropriate meals, for example halal, kosher, vegetarian, gluten free.
- Support all communication needs so that no one is excluded – for example, provide information in Braille, make hearing loops available, have staff available who can use sign language.
- Use non-discriminatory language – for example, call a service user by their preferred name, not 'dear' or 'love'.
- Avoid being patronising – for example when talking to young or older people.

> **Revision activity**
>
> Learn a range of examples of how practitioners in health and social care settings can apply each of the person-centred values of care. Make sure you can remember examples for each.
>
> You could make a set of revision cards: write the name of a person-centred value of care on the front of each card and on the back write a list of examples of it in practice.

> **Typical mistake**
>
> It is not correct to think that respecting people means to 'treat everyone the same'. People need to be treated differently according to their needs. For example, some people need, and get, more care, help and attention because of their physical or mental ability, condition or illness.

> **Exam tip**
>
> Examples can be interchangeable, particularly for respect/rights and for choice/individuality, but you will not get marks for repeats in the examination, so make sure you give different examples. Providing a prayer room is an example of a care setting respecting an individual's beliefs and this would gain the mark. However, it is also an example of how a care setting can value individuality, but you cannot gain the mark for the same example – you need to give a different one.

> **Now test yourself** TESTED
>
> 1. Define 'individuality'.
> 2. Give **two** examples of how staff at a retirement home could promote or support individuality.
> 3. Give **two** examples of how a care assistant could promote the independence of residents in their day-to-day work at a retirement home.
> 4. Identify **two** ways confidentiality could be maintained on a hospital ward.
> 5. Explain **two** ways staff at a residential care setting for young adults with learning disabilities could support their decision-making.
> 6. List **four** person-centred values of care applied in health and social care settings.

Qualities of a service practitioner, the 6Cs

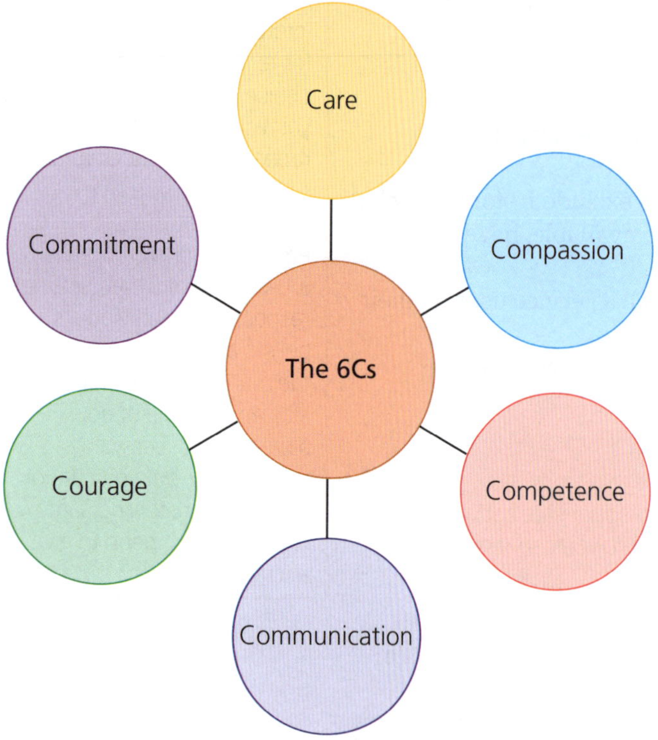

Figure 2.3 The 6Cs

The 6Cs are key principles which should inform every health and social care worker's practice:
- **Care** – a care worker should do all they can to maintain or improve an individual's health and well-being
- **Compassion** – being able to provide care and support with kindness, consideration, respect and empathy.
- **Competence** – the ability of a care worker to provide high-quality, effective and safe care and support with kindness, consideration, respect and empathy.
- **Communication** – essential to developing good relationships with service users, their families and also with colleagues. Being able to listen carefully and speak in a way that individuals receiving care and support can understand. (See also Topic area 3: Effective communication skills in health and social care settings.)
- **Courage** – being brave and able to speak up about concerns, doing the right thing and also having the courage to try something new, such as new ways of working.
- **Commitment** – a promise or agreement to do something. It is the responsibility that care workers and practitioners in health and social care services have for those in their care: to perform the tasks and carry out the responsibilities of their particular job role to the required standard and for the benefit of their service users.

> **Empathy** The ability to identify with another person's situation and understand how they may be feeling or thinking.

> **Exam tip**
> You need to be able to give examples of how care workers would use each of the 6Cs in their day-to-day work in care settings.

> **Revision activity**
> The Care Certificate sets out the standards that should be covered by induction training before members of the healthcare and social care support staff are allowed to work without direct supervision. The 6Cs form part of the overall standards.
> - Read about the '6Cs' and 'working in a person-centred way' using the link below and scrolling to '5. Work in a person centred way': (https://www.skillsforcare.org.uk/Developing-your-workforce/Care-Certificate/Care-Certificate-workbook.aspx).
> - Create a concept map about the 6Cs.

Exam-style question answers at www.hoddereducation.co.uk/myrevisionnotesdownloads

> **Typical mistakes**
>
> Avoid repeating the same example of applying the 6Cs. If you are asked for two or three examples, they must be different ones to gain the marks. You will not gain a mark for repetition.

> **Now test yourself** TESTED
>
> 1. List the 6Cs.
> 2. Write a definition of each of the 6Cs.
> 3. Give **two** examples of how a care assistant in a residential home could apply two of the 6Cs in their daily tasks.
> 4. Give **two** examples of how a practice nurse at a GP surgery could apply two of the 6Cs in their daily tasks.
> 5. Give **two** examples of how a worker in a homeless shelter could apply the 6Cs in their daily tasks.

2.2 Benefits of applying the person-centred values

Benefits for service providers of applying person-centred values

REVISED

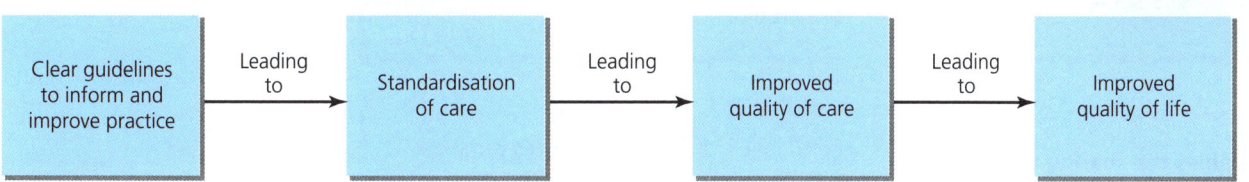

Figure 2.4 Impact of applying person-centred values of care

Applying the person-centred values of care has a big impact on the quality of care provided in care settings because service providers:
- have clear guidelines on the standards of care they need to provide
- experience improved job satisfaction
- can maintain and improve the quality of care they provide
- have their rights to choice and consultation supported
- can develop their skills
- share their good practice.

Benefits for service users of having the person-centred values applied

When the person-centred values are applied, service users will benefit.

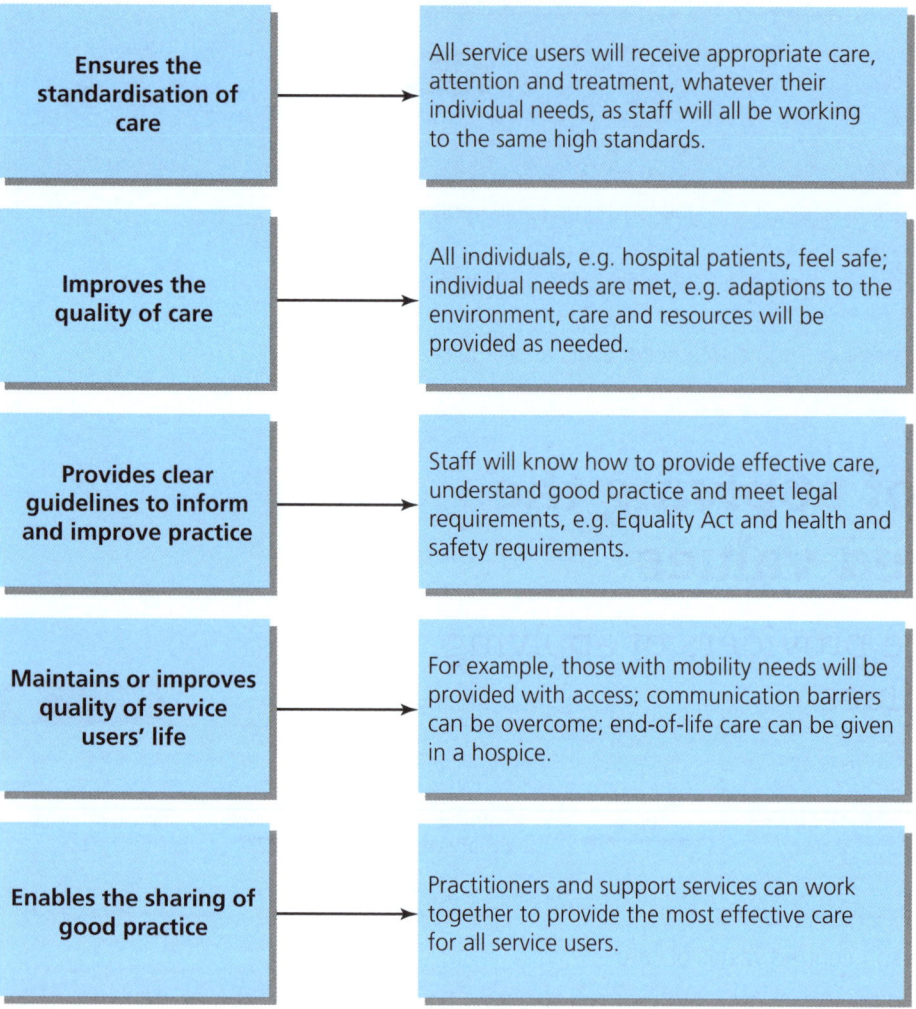

Figure 2.5 Benefits for service users when care workers apply person-centred values of care

Why it is important for care workers to apply the values of care

- To ensure the standardisation of care: all service users will be receiving appropriate care, attention and treatment whatever their individual needs; staff will all be working to the same high standards.
- To improve the quality of care: all individuals will feel safe; the service users' individual needs will be met through adaptations to the environment, and correct care and resources will be provided when needed.
- To provide clear guidelines to inform and improve practice: staff will know how to provide effective care; staff will receive guidance about legal requirements and good practice.

- To maintain or improve quality of life: for example, this could mean helping a patient to recover or be as comfortable and independent as possible; providing access for those with mobility problems or overcoming communication barriers; providing appropriate end-of-life care in a hospice.
- To support service users to develop their strengths: ensures the service user is involved in decision-making by discussing their care needs and then being given, for example, information about the different options that will meet their needs. This is enabling and empowering, ensuring the service user is at the centre of their care and has choice and control. Their rights to choice and consultation are supported.

Empowerment The process that enables individuals to take control of their lives and make their own decisions; giving someone confidence in their own abilities.

Revision activity

Choose ten points from the bullet list below. For each point explain a specific action that a care worker would carry out to demonstrate person-centred care.

Person-centred values of care in practice:
- all patients receiving the appropriate care and attention
- all individuals feeling safe
- individuals feel valued
- individuals are kept safe
- needs being met
- service users treated fairly
- special needs provided for
- promoting good relationships
- trust
- raising self-esteem
- raising self-confidence
- empowering individuals
- showing respect
- promoting rights
- being a role model – teaching others not to discriminate
- ensuring individuals don't feel stupid or patronised
- ensuring standardisation of care
- improving the quality of care
- providing clear guidelines to inform and improve practice
- maintaining or improving quality of life

Exam tip

Read the exam question carefully. Is it asking about applying person-centred values of care in a healthcare or a social care setting? Or is it asking for general points that could apply to both types of settings? Make sure you do what the question asks.

Typical mistake

Read the exam question carefully – is it asking for the benefits of applying person-centred values of care for service *providers* or service *users*? If you write about the wrong one, you will not gain any marks.

Now test yourself   TESTED

1. Give the meaning of the term 'empowerment'.
2. Describe **two** ways that staff applying the person-centred values of care can benefit a service user.
3. List **four** benefits for service providers of applying person-centred values of care.

2.3 Effects on service users' health and well-being if person-centred values are not applied

Examples of person-centred values of care not being applied include:
- incidents of inappropriate breaking of confidentiality – for example, staff gossiping about the patients, an individual's personal records left lying around
- equipment and aids not safety checked, not repaired, not PAT tested
- failure to carry out risk assessments
- no provision for special diets
- no provision for different cultures
- no provision for disabilities – learning, mobility, communication
- no safeguarding procedures
- no policies on, for example, health and safety, equal opportunities, bullying
- no planning or review of activities
- lack of communication with patients or other care professionals
- failure to challenge incidents of discrimination.

> **PAT tested** Stands for 'Portable Appliance Testing'; used to describe the checking of electrical appliances and equipment to ensure they are safe to use.

PIES

REVISED

Effects on individuals can be:

Physical

Intellectual

Emotional

Social.

> **Exam tip**
> It can help to remember these as the 'PIES' effects.

Physical effects of person-centred values not being applied

REVISED

Physical effects relate to an individual's body. Not applying the person-centred values of care may lead to poor physical health and well-being.

Some examples of possible physical effects are:
- dehydration if a person doesn't like drinking the tea or other drinks that they are given without consultation
- malnutrition and/or eating disorders – for example if an individual stops eating meals due to boredom or dislike of what is provided, or if inappropriate food is provided such as no vegetarian options or no gluten-free food for individuals with coeliac disease
- self-harm due to depression, lack of stimulation or social interaction, or mental health issues
- the individual's general health could deteriorate due to poor care – for example, they could become unfit and gain weight because they are not given opportunities to exercise or they lack energy for exercise due to a poor diet
- injuries such as cuts, grazes and bruises or even broken bones as the result of abusive treatment or poor manual handling by untrained care workers, or due to trip hazards and old equipment in need of repair
- existing illness could get worse without proper treatment or if medications are not given at the correct times.

Exam-style question answers at www.hoddereducation.co.uk/myrevisionnotesdownloads

Intellectual effects of person-centred values not being applied

REVISED

Intellectual means an individual's thought processes, such as thinking skills, understanding, learning, reasoning, comprehension and knowledge.

Some examples of possible intellectual effects if the person-centred values of care are not applied are outlined here.

Example 1

A 12 year-old with learning difficulties is having a poor experience at school. If they are not given enough support or if they are given learning activities which are not matched to their special needs, it could result in:
- lack of skills development – writing, reading, etc.
- not being able to communicate well, limited vocabulary
- lack of knowledge
- lack of progress, leading to restricted study and employment opportunities later in life
- lack of achievement
- failure to achieve potential – for example, may not get an interesting and rewarding job in the future.

Example 2

A care home resident experiences a lack of stimulation. For example, they are left in front of the television every day and this could result in:
- lack of mental engagement
- loss of focus/concentration
- lack of interest
- lack of motivation
- poor mental health, for example depression.

> **Exam tip**
>
> It is important to realise that effects do not occur in isolation but are interrelated (they affect one another). For example, a practitioner being bullied at work may suffer physical harm such as bruises. This could lead to them feeling unsafe, causing them to take time off work in order to avoid the bully. Not going to work could lead to a lack of career progress or losing their job.

> **Revision activity**
>
> Learn at least four effects for each of the PIES.

Emotional effects of person-centred values not being applied

REVISED

Emotional effects relate to an individual's feelings.
- If hospital patients are not consulted regarding their care, or if staff are too busy to answer their questions or explain treatments and medication, over time the emotional impacts can be significant.
- A young adult with special learning needs who is never praised for their work, or who is not helped when they are bullied, can suffer long-lasting and severe emotional distress.

Further examples of possible emotional effects on individuals if the person-centred values of care are not applied are outlined here.

Feeling disempowered

- Individuals experiencing disempowerment feel unwanted and unimportant.
- They may feel a lack of control over their life.
- Individuals become disengaged with life and lose interest.
- An individual may feel demoralised and not motivated to achieve.
- They may start to think that carers know best because their thoughts and feelings are ignored.
- An individual may accept whatever happens and no longer be bothered to complain.
- It may lead to behaviour changes – for example, they may become aggressive or uncooperative.

> **Disempowerment** Feeling that you have a lack of control over your life and lack independence.

- This may lead to loss of independence – for example, feeling they can't make decisions.
- An individual can be left feeling betrayed – for example, if their confidentiality is broken.

Loss of self-confidence

- A lack of support restricts opportunities available to individuals, which prevents them from gaining self-confidence and does not help to empower them.
- An individual could develop low self-esteem and feel they are not capable of achieving anything.
- They may feel frustrated because they are not allowed to do anything for themselves.
- It can result in learned helplessness and a loss of motivation.
- An individual may be scared to tell carers what they want or need.

> **Learned helplessness**
> When someone gives up trying as a result of consistent lack of achievement or reward – they come to believe that it is not worth trying because they will fail anyway.

Table 2.2 Emotional effects and their impact if the person-centred values of care are not applied

Emotional effects	Possible impacts on individuals
- Angry/annoyed/frustrated - Devalued - Embarrassed - Scared/frightened - Feel inadequate - Humiliation - Loss of trust - Low self-confidence - Low self-esteem - Feel unsafe - Stress - Unhappy and upset - Feelings of worthlessness	- Become withdrawn and do not want to join in with others - Do not want to attend the care setting, e.g. hospital, GP surgery, day centre - Develop behaviour problems - Become aggressive towards others; loss of trust - Increased risk of injuries, accidents - Loss of concentration, leading to lack of progress and underachieving - Failure to thrive, developmental delay (children)

Social effects of person-centred values not being applied

REVISED

If the values of care are not applied, it can have social effects on a person. These relate to an individual's relationship with others.

For example, a care home resident could become isolated and lonely if carers do not seem interested in her and just talk among themselves rather than engaging with her.

Examples of possible social effects if the person-centred values of care are not applied include:
- living alone and being socially isolated, feeling lonely
- becoming anti-social/social withdrawal
- behaviour problems
- social exclusion/feeling left out
- poor social skills/less sociable/not wanting to interact with/talk to others
- inability to make relationships
- lack of friends
- feeling marginalised
- being uncooperative
- refusing to go to the care service or even to go out at all.

> **Marginalised** Excluded from participating; feeling unimportant and not wanted by the majority of people.

Exam tip

- If an examination question asks about emotional and social effects, for example, make sure your answer covers both so that you can get the highest marks. You will only gain a maximum of half marks if you only write about emotional OR social effects.
- When an examination question asks you to 'explain effects', you need to write about physical, intellectual, emotional and social effects. Make sure you give examples for all four types of effects or you will not gain high marks.

Typical mistakes

Don't be vague if an examination question on effects requires a short answer. It is okay to answer with one word, but remember to be precise. For example, stating 'hurt' as an emotional effect is too vague – it could mean physically hurt or emotionally hurt; a better answer would be 'upset' or 'unhappy'.

Now test yourself   TESTED

1. State the meaning of the terms 'physical', 'intellectual', 'emotional' and 'social'.
2. Give **two** physical effects and **two** emotional effects on a hospital patient who is not given regular drinks and so does not get enough fluids.
3. Describe the emotional effects on a pregnant woman who is told, without any explanation, that she cannot have a home birth.
4. Jayson, age 17, is being bullied at the day centre. Explain the possible effects on him of being bullied.

Exam-style questions

1. State a definition of 'person-centred values' of care. [2]
2. Identify the 6Cs. [6]
3. The text below outlines the meaning of 'the 6Cs'. Complete the sentences using words from the list provided. Each word from the list may be used once only or not at all.

| needs | service users | guidelines | principles |
| working | preferences | care worker | decisions |

Person-centred values are key _____ that underpin the work of those providing care and support in health and social care services.

They are a set of _____ that provide ways of _____ for care settings and their staff.

Person-centred practice enables _____ to receive person-centred care that meets their own unique _____. [5]

4. Sundus is the practice manager at a local GP surgery. The surgery has received complaints from patients about being patronised and spoken to disrespectfully. Other complaints involved patients having to give personal information to the receptionist where everyone could overhear.

    Sundus arranges:
    - training about person-centred care, in particular respecting patients
    - a booklet for each member of staff about privacy and dignity.

    Evaluate how Sundus's actions could help the staff improve their practice. Your evaluation should include:
    - strengths of each of Sundus's actions
    - weaknesses of each of Sundus's actions. [8]

5. Fill in the following table by stating one correct person-centred value of care for each example. [4]

Examples of applying person-centred values of care	Person-centred value
A GP sharing a patient's personal information with a social worker.	
A social worker arranging for mobility aids to enable an elderly man to stay in his home rather than go to live in a care home.	
A social worker holding a case meeting with a family in an empty office, with the door closed.	
A manager of a foodbank ensuring that a range of food is available for individual needs, for example vegetarian, Halal, Kosher and gluten free.	

6. Describe **two** benefits for service providers of applying the person-centred values. [4]
7. Identify **two** benefits for service users of having the person-centred values applied. [2]
8. Explain ways that a social care worker could promote and value individuality in care settings. [8]
9. List **four** possible intellectual effects on a teenage girl who is being bullied because she misses school every Tuesday to go to the hospital for treatment for a condition she likes to keep private. [4]
10. Beth, an 88-year-old resident of a care home, is left watching TV all day and is allowed visitors only at weekends due to staff shortages.

    The person-centred values of care are not being applied at Beth's care home.

    Describe physical, emotional and social effects on Beth of the person-centred values of care not being applied. [6]

Topic area 3: Effective communication skills in health and social care settings

Communication is a two-way process of sharing messages with others using both verbal and non-verbal methods:
- Verbal communication is what we say to another person.
- Non-verbal communication is using body language, writing information or using specialist methods such as Braille.

Care practitioners should use effective communication skills, adapted for the individual's specific needs. This ensures that service users clearly understand the messages and information they share with them.

> **Body language** A type of non-verbal communication through body posture, facial expressions, gestures and eye contact.
>
> **Braille** A method of communication used by visually impaired or blind people that consists of raised dots which are read by touch.

3.1 The importance of verbal communication skills in health and social care settings

Verbal communication

REVISED

Verbal communication includes the spoken word and sound. For example:
- a conversation
- a phone call
- speaking one to one
- asking or answering questions
- discussing treatment
- a recorded message
- delivering a training session
- interviewing someone.

Adapting the type/method of communication to meet the needs of the service user or the situation

REVISED

In health and social care settings, practitioners have to use a range of communication skills in many different situations every day. Some examples of common situations include:
- finding out about a person's symptoms
- explaining test results
- giving bad news to a patient or their family
- consoling someone who is upset
- responding to questions
- responding to complaints
- calming someone down
- discussing individuals' treatment and progress with the care team.

It is very important that care practitioners have good communication skills and can adapt them to meet the needs of a wide range of different individuals. This enables them to establish good relationships with service users and their families, as well as with other staff.

Exam-style question answers at www.hoddereducation.co.uk/myrevisionnotesdownloads

Verbal communication skills

REVISED

It is important that you are aware of verbal communication skills:
- Clarity – information that is clearly stated and is understandable.
- Empathy – the ability to imagine yourself in another person's situation and understand how they might be thinking or feeling. This can help a care worker to gain a better understanding of another person and lets the service user know that their feelings have been acknowledged.
- Patience – not making a service user feel pressured, giving them the time to say what they need and want. Repeating if necessary so they can take in the information.
- Using appropriate vocabulary – straightforward medical or other information is given and any specialist terms are avoided, or if not they are explained in simplified everyday terms. Jargon that only health or social care professionals would understand is not used as far as possible.
- Tone – a positive and even tone of voice, which is not too loud or too quiet, is friendly, calm and reassuring.
- Volume – speaking too loudly can be assertive or domineering. It can also breach confidentiality if people can overhear. Choose a volume suitable to where the conversation is taking place and based on the situation; for example, speaking to a patient about test results or delivering a training session to a group of staff will require a different volume to be used.
- Pace – important information will be missed if a care worker speaks too quickly. For example, at a shift handover on a hospital ward, it is vital that the health and progress of all patients is clearly understood by the incoming staff, so this should not be rushed. It is important to use an appropriate pace that gives others enough time to take in information or instructions.
- Willingness to contribute to team working – teams of staff do not always work together face to face; they can communicate with each other through conference calls, patient records, emails and telephone calls. This enables the necessary information to be shared.

> **Jargon** Specialist or technical language or terms and abbreviations that are difficult for non-specialists to understand.

Exam tip
Make sure that you know a range of verbal and non-verbal communication skills and can give examples of situations when they would be used.

Revision activity
For each of the communication skills listed and described above, describe an example of a situation where a care practitioner would use each of the skills.

Now test yourself
TESTED

1. Name **four** different types of verbal communication skills.
2. Explain each skill you named in question 1.
3. Describe **two** ways that care workers might use their verbal communication skills in a care setting.
4. Give **three** situations where care workers would need to adapt their method of communication.

Topic area 3: Effective communication skills in health and social care settings

37

Cambridge National Level 1/2 Health and Social Care

3.2 The importance of non-verbal communication skills in health and social care settings

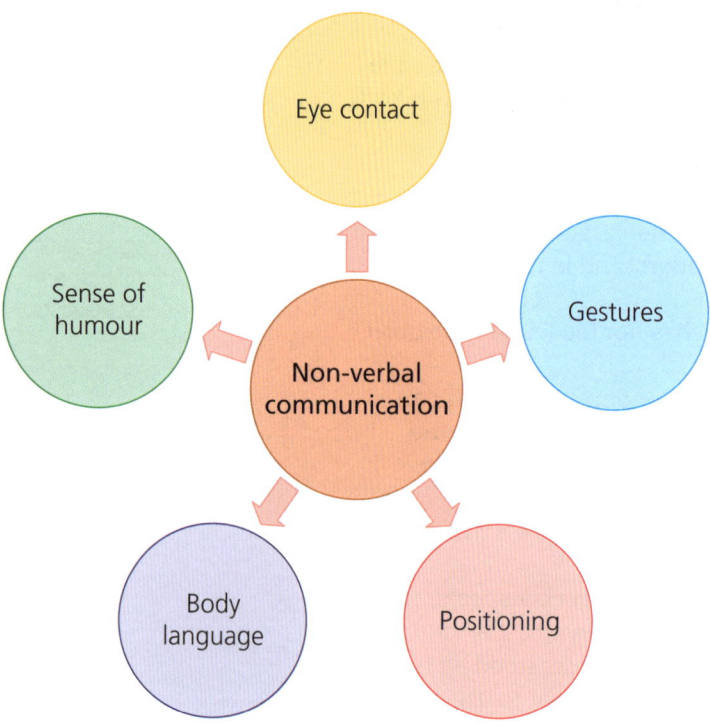

Figure 3.1 Types of non-verbal communication

Non-verbal communication is when someone's behaviour and appearance send messages about how they feel. This could be through facial expressions or body language, for example, or any of the factors shown in Figure 3.1. All of these factors can have a positive or negative effect on the communication taking place.

Examples of non-verbal communication

REVISED

- Eye contact – showing interest, acknowledging what has been said.
- Gestures – thumbs up or down, wave hello/goodbye, pointing something out.
- Facial expression – interested, reassurance, agreement.
- Body language – positive/open, no crossed arms or legs.
- Sense of humour – being able to see the funny side of things.

Positioning

REVISED

If not thought through, this can create physical and emotional barriers that inhibit effective communication. If a service user cannot see the care worker properly because of where they are standing, it does not support good communication. Emotionally, having someone leaning over and looking down on them can make a service user feel insignificant and powerless because they feel dominated.

- Space and personal space – ideally meetings should take place in a room where there is enough space for everyone to sit down and feel comfortable, and for them to be facing each other so that facial expressions and body language can be observed. It is important that people do not have to sit too closely together as they may feel their personal space is being invaded. This will have a negative effect on the communication taking place.

Exam-style question answers at www.hoddereducation.co.uk/myrevisionnotesdownloads

- Height – ideally, a person will be at the same level as the practitioner who is talking with them. If the practitioner, for example a social worker, is standing and the service user is sitting, they may feel dominated by the social worker, as though they are being talked down to. This does not help effective communication.

Figure 3.2 Using non-verbal communication skills

> **Revision activity**
> - Look carefully at Figure 3.2.
> - Describe the non-verbal communication skills that are being used.

> **Exam tip**
>
> Make sure that you know, and can describe, different ways of communicating non-verbally with a range of service users in different situations.

> **Typical mistake**
>
> Don't mix up verbal and non-verbal communication. Make sure you read the question carefully and provide an answer that is about the correct method.
>
> Remember, verbal communication involves sounds and speech, non-verbal is body language and unspoken messages.

> **Now test yourself** TESTED
>
> 1 List **five** types of non-verbal communication, giving an example for each.
> 2 Why are positioning and height important when speaking with a service user?
> 3 How is having a sense of humour a useful aspect of effective communication?

Cambridge National Level 1/2 Health and Social Care

3.3 The importance of active listening skills in health and social care settings

Active listening is an effective method of listening to build rapport, trust and understanding between those involved. The use of active listening by a care practitioner involves demonstrating an interest in and responsiveness to what a person is saying – it shows they are fully concentrating on what is being said rather than just passively 'hearing'.

Active listening can involve non-verbal cues which show understanding, such as nodding, eye contact and briefly saying 'I see' or 'sure', for example, to build trust and confidence.

Active listening skills

REVISED

Successful active listening needs to follow these stages, in this order:
- Open, relaxed posture.
- Eye contact, looking interested.
- Nodding agreement.
- Showing empathy, reflecting feelings.
- Clarifying.
- Summarising to show understanding of key points.

> **Posture** The position in which someone holds their body when standing or sitting.

Figure 3.3 Active listening skills in practice

Exam-style question answers at www.hoddereducation.co.uk/myrevisionnotesdownloads

> **Revision activity**
>
> Consider the picture in Figure 3.3, which shows a care assistant chatting with a care home resident. Identify how the care assistant is using effective communication with the resident and explain the benefits.
>
> Think about body language, facial expression, gestures, positioning and active listening.

Benefits of practitioners using active listening skills

REVISED

Table 3.1 Benefits of active listening

For service users	For practitioners
They will feel secure that the service provider has listened and is aware of the type of care they need.	Helps them to gather information needed to inform the type of care required.
They will feel respected as individuals.	Helps them to get to know the individual.
They will feel empowered as they will have had the opportunity to express their needs, worries and preferences.	They will be aware of the service user's needs, preferences and choices.
Establishes co-operation, trust and involvement in a care partnership.	Allows carers to identify and plan to meet the individual's needs.

> **Exam tip**
>
> Ensure that you are clear about the definition of the stages of active listening. Take care to use the correct wording in the answers that you give.

> **Typical mistake**
>
> Don't get the stages of active listening in the wrong order. The stages follow a sequence, so you need to know and memorise the correct order.

> **Now test yourself** TESTED
>
> 1 Write a definition of active listening in your own words.
> 2 List the **six** active listening skills in the correct order.
> 3 How do practitioners benefit from using active listening?
> 4 How do service users benefit from practitioners using active listening?

3.4 The importance of special methods of communication in health and social care settings

Advocate

REVISED

Health and social care services can support certain individuals' rights by providing an advocate. An advocate is someone who speaks on behalf of an individual who is unable to speak up for themselves.

Figure 3.4 An advocate speaks on behalf of someone who is unable to do so for themselves

Who might need an advocate?

Individuals who could need an advocate include:
- a young child
- someone with a learning disability
- an older person with a condition such as Alzheimer's
- someone who has been assessed as lacking mental capacity
- people with mental health problems
- someone with a physical disability.

Examples of what an advocate can do

An advocate can:
- go with an individual to meetings or attend for them
- help an individual to find and access information
- write letters on the individual's behalf
- speak on behalf of someone at a case conference to express their wishes.

Table 3.2 The role of an advocate

An advocate will:	An advocate will not:
• be completely independent and represent the individual's views, not their own opinions • ensure an individual's rights and needs are recognised • represent the individual's wishes and views • speak on behalf of someone someone who is unable to do so for themselves • act in the best interests of the person they are representing.	• judge the individual • give their personal opinion • make decisions for the individual.

Example situations where an advocate can help

- A member of the community mental health team represents an 18-year-old individual with learning difficulties who wants to leave home and live in supported housing, to ensure the individual's rights are maintained.
- Using a volunteer from a charity such as MIND to help with an application for disability benefits to ensure the individual's rights and entitlements are supported.
- A family friend represents an older person with dementia by speaking about their needs with a hospital social worker when a care plan is being discussed. This ensures their best interests are supported.

> **Exam tip**
>
> Make sure that you can write a definition of advocacy and can give an example of how it can support an individual's rights.

> **Typical mistake**
>
> Don't state that advocates 'speak for' someone. This is inaccurate. Advocates represent the views and preferences of an individual – they speak on their behalf, not 'for' them.

> **Revision activity**
>
> Draw a grid with four rows and four columns. Fill in each box with a fact about advocacy.

> **Now test yourself** TESTED
>
> 1 Give an example of a situation where a teenager might need an advocate.
> 2 Give **three** practical examples of what an advocate could do when representing someone.
> 3 How does advocacy support an individual's rights?
> 4 List **three** things an advocate will not do.

Special methods of communicating

- **Braille** – Braille consists of a series of dots which are read by touch. Each character is made up of raised dots; the raised dots may be in any of six positions within a rectangle. There are 64 possible combinations of dots.
- **British Sign Language (BSL)** – uses hand signs, facial expressions and gestures to make visual signs to communicate with individuals who have impaired hearing.
- **Hearing loop** – a special type of sound system for use by people with hearing aids. The hearing loop provides a wireless signal that is picked up by the hearing aid and can greatly improve the quality of sound while reducing background noise.
- **Interpreter** – converts a spoken or signed message from one language to another.
- **Makaton** – uses gestures alongside symbols/pictures and speech.
- **PECS** – picture exchange communication – uses pictures that aid communication. It is a specialist method of communication developed for use with children who have autism. It helps them learn to start communicating by exchanging a picture for the item or activity that they want.

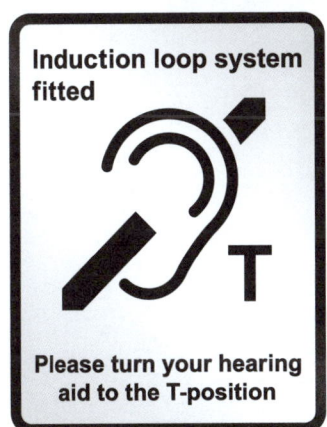

Figure 3.5 Adapting the environment to improve access to health and social care services could include installing a hearing loop for individuals who are deaf or hearing impaired

- **Translator** – converts a written message from one language to another.
- **Voice-activated software** – speech-activated programs allow users to write text, use the internet, send email and use applications with their voice rather than a mouse or keyboard. These programs can be very helpful to people who do not have full use of their hands and therefore have difficulty using a keyboard and mouse.
  - **Dynavox** – speech-generating software. Through touching a screen that contains text, pictures and symbols, the software then converts those symbols into speech.
  - **Lightwriter** – a text-to-speech device. A message is typed on a keyboard, is displayed on the screen and then converted into speech.

> **Revision activity**
>
> Create a concept map of specialist methods of communication and extend it by adding the benefits of each method for individuals.

> **Typical mistake**
>
> Don't confuse an interpreter or translator with someone who uses sign language.

> **Exam tip**
>
> You should be able to suggest ways of communicating effectively with a range of service users. For example:
> - young children
> - someone with learning difficulties
> - an individual who is blind or hearing impaired
> - someone who does not speak the same language as the care provider
> - someone who is upset and distressed
> - an older person with dementia
> - other care workers in the setting.

> **Now test yourself**
>
> 1. Give **two** examples for each of non-verbal communication and verbal communication.
> 2. Describe ways of communicating effectively with an individual who has dementia.
> 3. Explain how effective communication supports individual rights.
> 4. Suggest ways a practice nurse could communicate effectively with a patient who only speaks Polish.

Exam-style question answers at www.hoddereducation.co.uk/myrevisionnotesdownloads

3.5 The importance of effective communication in health and social care settings

The impact of good communication skills

REVISED

Effective communication supports the person-centred values and protects individual rights by helping to meet service users' individual needs.

Table 3.3 The importance of effective communication

Examples of effective communication methods	How they support rights and person-centred values
Using appropriate vocabulary	• Aids service user's understanding of treatments or procedures and reassures them. • No jargon or specialist terminology that could be confusing. • Enables informed decisions to be made.
Not being patronising	• Service users feel valued and respected. • Instils confidence. • Develops trust. • Reassures service users they are being taken seriously.
Adapting communication, e.g. by emphasising words/slowing the pace/varying tone/using gestures	• Meets the needs of the individual or the situation. • Equality of access. • The service user will understand and so can make informed choices.
Listening to individual's needs/active listening	• Empowers; individuals feel valued and respected. • Raises self-esteem. • Instils confidence. • Shows care workers are listening.
Use of aids – for example, installing a hearing loop system	• Ensures equality of access to services. • Empowers service users. • Individual needs are met.
Using specialist methods, for example using sign language or PECS	
Interpreters or leaflets in other languages	
Information in a variety of formats, for example large print, Braille	

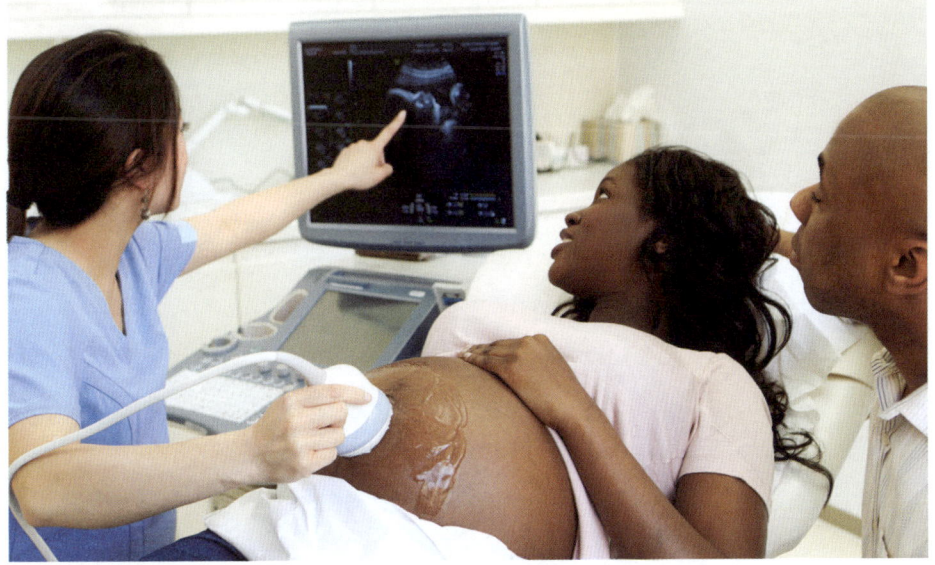

Figure 3.6 A sonographer using effective communication skills

> **Revision activity**
>
> The **sonographer** shown in Figure 3.6 is using a range of communication skills.
>
> Make a list of the different communication skills and for each one state why it promotes effective communication.

> **Sonographer** A health professional who is specially trained to carry out ultrasound scans.

Overcoming barriers to communication

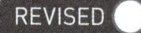

- Actively listening to the individual about their communication needs/preferences – this reassures them that they are valued and respected.
- Active involvement from the individual – ask them how/when/where and in which way they like to be communicated with to meet their needs; this shows respect for the individual and their needs.
- Access to information that is understandable to the particular individual – in the correct language, or using a special method, with no specialist terminology; so they are well informed about their care or treatment.
- Choice of communication aids or support that matches the needs and preferences of the individual; this will support successful and effective communication with the individual.
- Access to a range of support options and personal choice given to individual – respects individual's rights.

Table 3.4 Ways of communicating effectively

Using vocabulary that can be understood by all	<ul><li>Avoid jargon.</li><li>Explain any specialist terminology.</li><li>Use age-appropriate vocabulary.</li><li>Use simplified language, for example with young children, individuals with learning disabilities or patients with dementia.</li><li>Use interpreters or translators.</li></ul>
Use communication that is appropriate to the individual	<ul><li>Use positive body language, such as nodding agreement and making eye contact.</li><li>Avoid sarcasm and do not talk down to the person.</li><li>Be polite.</li><li>Make the service user feel they are being taken seriously.</li><li>Be patient, especially when listening to repetition.</li><li>Do not ignore the person's views or beliefs just because they are different from yours.</li></ul>
Listen to individuals' needs/active listening	<ul><li>Use active listening by demonstrating interest in response to what a person is saying, using body language to show a positive reaction.</li><li>Ask the person rather than assuming you know what they want, need or prefer.</li><li>Concentrate on what the person is saying – this can encourage them to communicate their needs.</li></ul>
Adapt communication to meet individuals' needs or the situation	<ul><li>Emphasise important words.</li><li>Slow the pace of conversation if necessary.</li><li>Increase the tone of voice but do not shout.</li><li>Use repetition where appropriate.</li><li>Using gestures or flash cards/pictures if appropriate.</li><li>Make use of aids to communication such as a hearing loop system.</li><li>Use specialist communication methods such as Braille or signing.</li><li>Use technological aids, such as Dynavox or a Lightwriter.</li></ul>

The impact of poor communication skills

REVISED

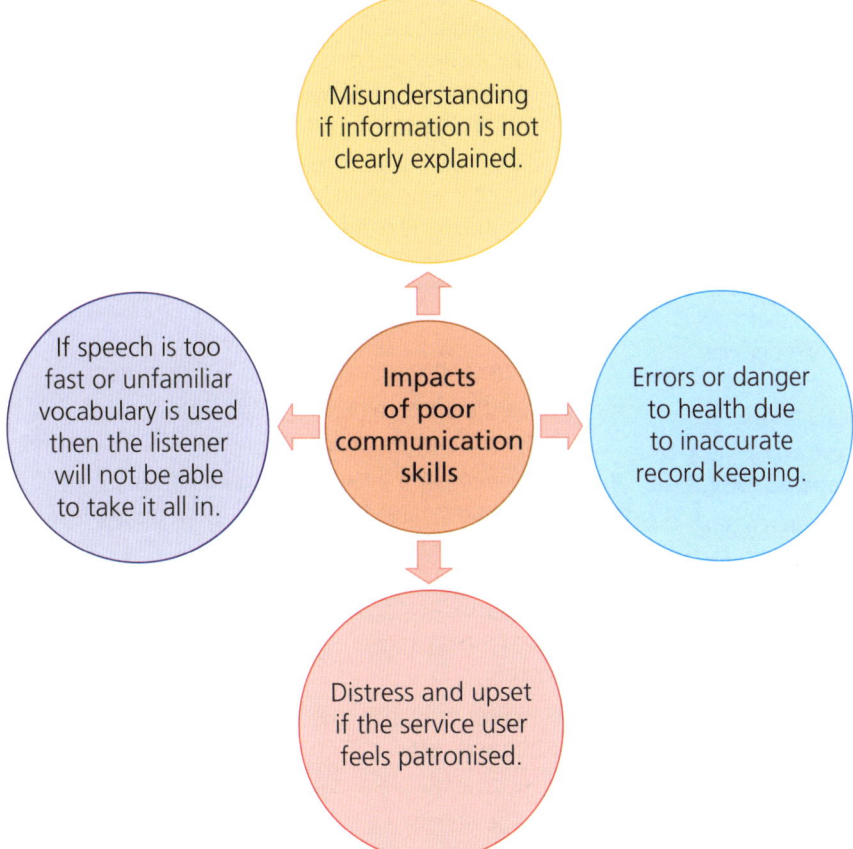

Figure 3.7 Impacts of poor communication skills

> **Revision activity**
>
> Ask a friend or relative about any contact they have had with health or social care services. What types of communication were used?
>
> How effective were the methods of communication used? What was good and what could be improved?

If communication is poor, many individuals, in particular those such as the groups listed below, will not have all the information they need or may not understand it because it has not been shared in an appropriate way.

Be particularly aware of individuals:
- with a learning disability
- with a physical disability
- who have had a stroke
- who have a hearing or visual impairment
- who speak a different language from the care providers
- who are shy and introverted and who may not enjoy communicating information with new staff.

It is important that the method of communication is adapted to ensure that their needs can be met.

> **Exam tip**
>
> When answering exam questions that require you to 'explain' you should:
> - give reasons – 'because' is a very useful word
> - state 'what' and 'why' in your answer.

> **Now test yourself** TESTED
>
> 1 Give **three** ways of adapting communication to meet individuals' needs.
> 2 Identify **three** methods of effective communication. For each, state how it supports rights and person-centred values.
> 3 Give **three** impacts of poor communication skills.
> 4 Identify groups of individuals who may not understand communication that is poor.

> **Typical mistake**
>
> Don't just state 'use appropriate vocabulary' without giving examples of what this means. You should be able to explain that this means not using jargon, technical terms or specialist medical terminology, for example.

Exam-style questions

1. Care workers should use 'appropriate vocabulary' when communicating with service users.

   State **three** examples of using appropriate vocabulary. [3]

2. Give **three** non-verbal communication skills that might be used by a school nurse when talking to a teenager. [3]

3. Communication at a GP surgery is poor.

   Impacts of poor communication are listed in the table below. Complete the table with an example of a possible cause for each impact. The first one has been done for you. [3]

Examples of poor communication	Impacts of poor communication
Information is not clearly explained; understanding not checked.	Patient misunderstands the treatment she is going to have
	Error or danger to health
	Distress or upset
	Inadequate information

4. A social worker is talking with an individual about changes to their care plan. During the conversation, which started in a very relaxed manner, the social worker notices that the person is getting fidgety and is avoiding eye contact. Their body language changes and they turn sideways on their chair so they no longer face the social worker.

   Analyse the situation and write **three** possible reasons for the individual's change in behaviour and body language. [3]

5. A social worker is talking with an individual about changes to their care plan. During the conversation, which started in a very relaxed manner, the social worker notices that the person is getting fidgety and is avoiding eye contact. Their body language changes and they turn sideways on their chair so they no longer face the social worker.

   Describe **three** actions you would take, based on the individual's body language and non-verbal communication messages, to find out what is bothering them about the meeting. [6]

6. A health and social care student has a work placement in a residential care home. Many of the residents have dementia, a condition that causes memory loss, confusion and difficulty with daily living tasks such as getting dressed and remembering to eat.

   Describe how these two ways of adapting the method of communication could be used by the student to help support the rights of the residents with dementia:
   - not being patronising
   - adapting communication to meet an individual's needs. [6]

7. One of the active listening skills is 'summarising'.

   Analyse the purpose of a nurse 'summarising' a conversation with a patient. [6]

8. Identify whether the following statements about the role of an advocate are true or false. Tick (✓) the box to show your answer. [5]

Role of an advocate	True	False
1 Gives their personal opinion.		
2 Represents an individual's wishes and views.		
3 Acts in the best interests of the person they are representing.		
4 Makes decisions for an individual.		
5 Helps service users to understand their rights.		

9. a State **one** communication problem that may occur for Liz, who has hearing loss, when she is attending a clinic appointment. [1]

   b Identify **three** methods that could be used to improve communication with practitioners at the clinic who are caring for individuals with hearing loss. [3]

10. Ash is a social worker. He works with children who have been taken into care. When he meets a child for the first time, they are often very frightened and upset.

    Explain how Ash can use effective communication skills to ensure the children's rights are maintained. [8]

Exam-style question answers at www.hoddereducation.co.uk/myrevisionnotesdownloads

Topic area 4: Protecting service users and service providers in health and social care settings

4.1 Safeguarding

Safeguarding means the measures taken to protect people's health, well-being and rights. This enables them to be kept safe from harm, abuse and neglect. Practitioners in health and social care organisations must all be aware of the need for safeguarding.

All health and social care services and care professionals have a duty to safeguard all service users and protect their human rights. It is a key aspect of providing high-quality person-centred care in the health and care sector and must be taken seriously as a responsibility.

Service users who need safeguarding

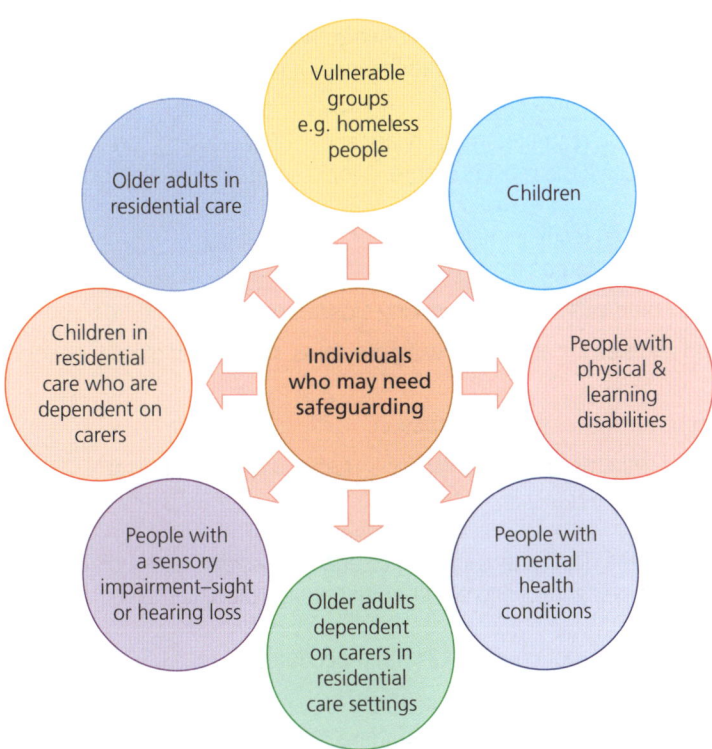

Figure 4.1 Individuals who may need safeguarding

Some individuals may be more at risk of abuse, maltreatment or neglect than others. Examples include individuals who:
- have a learning or physical disability
- have a sensory impairment (visually or hearing impaired)
- lack mental capacity due to dementia or being unresponsive, for example in a coma
- are homeless.

> **Sensory impairment**
> When one of the senses (sight, hearing, smell, touch, taste and spatial awareness) does not function normally. For example, if you wear glasses then you have sight impairment; if you wear a hearing aid then you have a hearing impairment.

Cambridge National Level 1/2 Health and Social Care

For many reasons these individuals may not want to, or may be unable to, report poor care or abuse. They:
- are dependent on carers and may not want to upset them in case their treatment gets worse
- may not know or understand their rights
- possibly may not even realise they are being abused
- may not see or hear who is abusing them.

Care workers have a duty of care to report concerns of suspected abuse or poor care to the organisation's safeguarding lead.

It is important to remember that while some service users may be more vulnerable to abuse or harm than others because of their individual needs or circumstances, anyone can potentially be at risk of abuse or harm.

Remember too that practitioners may be vulnerable, for example to bullying or unfair treatment in the workplace.

> **Vulnerable** When someone is less able to protect themselves from harm due to, for example, mental health problems or a physical or learning disability.

Common safeguarding issues in adult care environments

There are common safeguarding issues in adult care environments, all of which have an impact on service users.

Table 4.1 Some common safeguarding issues in adult care environments and their impacts

Safeguarding issue	Impacts
Maladministration of medication	• Incorrect, late or inappropriate medication, e.g. when administering sedatives or pain relief. • This can result in unrelieved pain and suffering, slow recovery or further illness if medication is inappropriate.
Inadequate care and neglect	• Individuals who are frail or who have restricted mobility are at risk of developing sores on the points of their body which receive the most pressure. People need to be moved often to avoid sores developing. • Lack of regular meals and drinks can result in malnutrition and dehydration. • Rough treatment, or being rushed, shouted at or ignored.
Falls	• Residents not being assessed on their risk of falls; walking aids not provided.
Poor nutritional care	• Inappropriate food provided for chewing and swallowing problems, religious or dietary needs, resulting in malnutrition.
Lack of social inclusion	• No stimulation, activity, opportunities for social interaction.

Institutional abuse	• Occurs when the routines and systems of an organisation result in poor or inadequate standards of care and poor practice.
	• This affects the whole setting:
	  • It denies, restricts or ignores the dignity, privacy, choice and independence of individuals.
	  • An example would be people being forced to eat or go to bed at a particular time in a residential home.
	  • Verbal abuse if the individual does not co-operate with procedures.

Physical abuse	• Between residents, or between staff and residents.
Financial abuse	• For example, theft of personal money or possessions, staff inappropriately accepting gifts.

Common safeguarding issues for children

These involve:
- protecting children from maltreatment – e.g. physical, emotional, psychological abuse
- preventing impairment of children's health and development – physical health and well-being, education
- ensuring children grow up in a stable home with the provision of safe and effective care – removal from neglect, unstable and chaotic family life
- taking action to enable all children to have the best outcomes – provision of support for the family, fostering or adoption.

Exam-style question answers at www.hoddereducation.co.uk/myrevisionnotesdownloads

The likelihood of abuse and harm

Abuse and harm are more likely to occur if:
- **equipment is old and/or damaged**, e.g. hoists, toys, and so could cause injury
- **activities and visits are not risk assessed** so potential risks and ways of avoiding them are not identified
- **staff are not trained in how to use equipment** and so may injure themselves or those in their care, e.g. when transferring someone out of a bath using a hoist
- **staff are not trained in how to carry out manual handling safely** and so may injure someone they are caring for, or themselves, while helping them out of bed into a chair, for example
- **staff are not trained in providing intimate care**, e.g. bathing, changing continence pads, etc., and so may be accused of abuse due to not following correct procedures
- there is a **shortage of staff** so they are rushed and unable to take the time required with their service users, who are then neglected, or staff may get impatient and use verbal abuse if, for example, someone with dementia is taking 'too long' to answer a care worker's questions
- there is a **lack of diversity and equality training** so incidents involving prejudice and discrimination are more likely to occur
- **staff are not given safeguarding training** and so are unaware of their role in dealing with suspected abuse or harm
- **staff are not DBS checked** and so it is not known if they have a criminal record and have been barred from working with vulnerable adults and children. If so, they may be a risk to individuals in their care.

> **Revision activity**
>
> Make sure you understand the meaning of 'safeguarding'.
>
> Safeguarding involves the responsibility to take proactive measures in order to reduce the risks for individuals of danger, harm and/or abuse.
>
> Create a concept map for all the information you know about safeguarding.

Figure 4.2 Staff must be given training in how to use a hoist safely. This is essential to avoid injury

> **Now test yourself** — TESTED
>
> 1 Identify **six** vulnerable groups of people who might be at risk of abuse or harm.
> 2 Give a reason, for each group you named in question 1, that explains why they might be more at risk.
> 3 Give **three** examples of common safeguarding issues for children.
> 4 Describe **three** examples of common safeguarding issues in adult care environments.
> 5 Describe **three** situations where abuse is more likely to occur.

Impacts for service users of a lack of safeguarding

REVISED

Remember PIES:
- Physical impacts – these relate to effects on an individual's body.
- Intellectual impacts – these relate to an individual's thought processes such as thinking skills, understanding, learning, comprehension and knowledge.
- Emotional impacts – these relate to an individual's feelings.
- Social impacts – these relate to an individual's relationship to others.

See also some further detailed examples of impacts in Topic area 2.3: Effects on service users' health and well-being if person-centred values are not applied on page 32.

Revision activity

Create a table with four columns and ten rows. Use the following headings:

Physical impacts	Intellectual impacts	Emotional impacts	Social impacts

Complete the columns of the table by adding examples of impacts due to a lack of safeguarding.

Here are some impacts that you can add to the table to get you started:

anxiety	injury	lack of understanding	disempowered
losing concentration	depression	fear	not trusting others
aggression	lack of motivation	bruising	withdrawn
uncooperative	poor mental health	self-harm	lack of interest in anything
pressure sores	despair	dehydration	stress

Fill in as many possible impacts of a lack of safeguarding as you can. Then share with a friend to fill in any gaps together.

Exam tip

Remember these impacts as '**PIES**' impacts: **P**hysical, **I**ntellectual, **E**motional and **S**ocial.

Typical mistake

If an exam question asks about emotional and social impacts, for example, make sure your answer covers both so you can get the highest marks. You will only be able to gain a maximum of half marks if you only write about 'emotional' OR 'social' impacts.

Exam tip

When an exam question asks you to 'explain effects' or 'give the impact of…', you need to write about physical, intellectual, emotional and social effects/impacts.

Make sure you give examples for each of the four types of effects. If you don't, you will limit the number of marks you can gain.

Safeguarding procedures in care settings

REVISED

Safeguarding policy

- All care settings are required by law to have safeguarding policies and procedures in place.
- The policy must state the ways of working and procedures to follow regarding any safeguarding issues.
- All staff must be trained so they are familiar with the policy and so they are aware of what to do if anyone makes a disclosure of abuse.

The need for safeguarding

Care settings need to follow safeguarding procedures in order to protect their service users and staff.

All care environments must have safeguarding procedures in place:
- They must have a specific person with responsibility for safeguarding.
- All staff and service users should be aware of the procedures to follow to report safeguarding issues.
- Staff should know how to deal with disclosures of abuse.

> **Disclosure** When an individual tells you directly, or indirectly through their behaviour, that they have been, or are being, abused.
>
> **CQC** Care Quality Commission – a government organisation that registers, licenses and inspects health and social care services.

Designated Safeguarding Lead (DSL)

The DSL is the person in an organisation, or service, that has overall responsibility for safeguarding.

The role of the DSL includes:
- creating the care setting's safeguarding policy
- reviewing the setting's plan for safeguarding
- ensuring all staff know how to raise safeguarding concerns
- referring concerns over an individual's welfare to social services, police, the CQC or other appropriate organisation
- providing training so all staff understand the signs and symptoms of abuse and neglect
- gathering any evidence or information about incidents of abuse or neglect.

Safeguarding training for all staff

REVISED

All staff, care workers and other staff, regardless of their job role, must be trained in safeguarding. They should receive regular refresher training to stay up to date in safeguarding procedures. It is compulsory for all those who come into contact with children and vulnerable adults in their work.

Figure 4.3 Staff should attend refresher safeguarding training regularly

Cambridge National Level 1/2 Health and Social Care

Some organisations use the 'five Rs' to help train staff to develop awareness of their responsibilities regarding safeguarding. This also helps to prepare them for a situation where harm or abuse is disclosed.

The five Rs are:
- Recognise
- Respond
- Report
- Record
- Refer.

Table 4.2 explains how to put the five Rs into practice when dealing with a safeguarding issue.

Table 4.2 What are the five Rs and what do they mean in practice?

The five Rs	What the five Rs mean in practice
Recognise	• Staff should be able to recognise the signs and symptoms of abuse or harm. • However, sometimes it may be a direct disclosure from an individual.

Respond	• Follow these steps:
	  • Listen to the disclosure – do not ask questions.
	  • Write it down as soon as possible, in the person's own words.
	  • Reassure the individual they've done the right thing.
	  • Inform them you will write down what they have said and will pass it on so that the abuse/harm can be dealt with, on a 'need-to-know' basis.

Report	• Report the concern to the Designated Safeguarding Lead member of staff. • It is then their responsibility to take appropriate action.
Record	• The DSL will record the concern raised, using direct quotes of exactly what was said, where possible. • If relevant, notes will be made about the individual's physical and emotional state that the DSL has observed.
Refer	• The DSL will investigate the allegations, complaints or suspicions of abuse. • If a crime is suspected, the DSL will contact the police.

> **Exam tip**
>
> Memorise the five Rs. This will enable you to write a complete description of the safeguarding procedures that have to be followed.

> **Revision activity**
>
> Create a spider diagram of the role of the DSL. Extend it with an explanation of what each aspect of the role requires.

> **Now test yourself** TESTED
>
> 1. Give **three** reasons why it is important for all care settings to have a safeguarding policy.
> 2. What does DSL stand for?
> 3. Describe the role of the DSL.
> 4. What are the 'five Rs'?
> 5. List **three** things you should do if someone tells you they have been harmed.

Exam-style question answers at www.hoddereducation.co.uk/myrevisionnotesdownloads

Disclosure and Barring Service

DBS checks ensure that individuals are safe to work or volunteer with vulnerable adults and children. The checks prevent anyone who is not suitable from working with individuals who have support needs such as learning disabilities or dementia, or who need health or personal care, for example.

- Disclosure and Barring Service checks are a requirement for anyone over 16 for roles that involve working or volunteering with children or vulnerable adults.
- This also applies to anyone applying to foster or adopt a child.

There are three types of DBS checks and a 'barred list':

- standard – checks for criminal convictions, cautions, reprimands and final warnings
- enhanced – an additional check of any information held by police that is relevant to the role being applied for
- enhanced with list checks – additionally checks the 'barred list'
- barred list – a list of individuals who are on record as being unsuitable to work with children or vulnerable adults. Therefore they are 'barred' – that is, not allowed to do this kind of work.

Figure 4.4 The Disclosure and Barring Service checks staff and volunteers are suitable to work in care settings. An organisation may use unofficial symbols like this to confirm their staff have been checked.

> **Exam tip**
>
> Make sure you know what the initials 'DBS' stand for and what the service does.

> **Revision activity**
>
> Find out more about the role of the DBS on its website: About us – Disclosure and Barring Service – GOV.UK (**www.gov.uk**).

> **Now test yourself** TESTED
>
> 1. What is the purpose of DBS checks?
> 2. State **two** groups of people who would need to have DBS checks.
> 3. Name the three types of DBS check.
> 4. Describe each of the three types of DBS check.
> 5. What is the 'barred list'?

4.2 Infection prevention

General cleanliness

REVISED

Different care settings will have different types of furniture and equipment. Therefore, the methods of maintaining general cleanliness will vary depending on the setting and the type of care services provided.

Some examples of ways to maintain a high standard of general cleanliness are listed below.

General cleanliness in healthcare settings

- Clear spillages, for example vomit, urine or blood, straight away and then clean and disinfect the area.
- Sterilise surgical equipment after use.
- Dispose of hazardous waste following correct procedures – for example, dispose of hospital sharps and cannulas in a hard yellow sharps box.
- Use specialist disposal methods such as red laundry bags for soiled bed linen, yellow bags for used dressings, disposable gloves and other clinical waste.
- Clean and disinfect bathrooms and toilets frequently (at least once daily).
- All used antiseptic wipes and tissues should be disposed of immediately after use into a covered bin.

Sharps Examples include used needles and cannulas (see below).

Cannulas Thin tubes that surround a flexible needle that is inserted into a vein to administer medication from a drip.

Figure 4.5 Thorough cleaning is a high priority in care settings to help prevent the spread of infection

General cleanliness in social care settings

- Mop floors and vacuum carpets every day.
- Wash work surfaces with hot soapy water.
- Use bins with lids – bins should be emptied and cleaned frequently.
- Clean and disinfect bathrooms and toilets frequently, at least daily.
- Wash bedding and towels regularly. Put soiled bedding into special red laundry bags.
- Wash curtains, blinds and soft furnishings, such as cushion covers, regularly.
- Clean toys and play equipment regularly.
- Dust coffee tables, dining tables and chairs regularly.
- TV remote controls and computer keyboards should be cleaned using anti-bacterial spray.

Exam-style question answers at www.hoddereducation.co.uk/myrevisionnotesdownloads

How this helps to prevent the spread of infection

- Prevents transfer of bacteria from surfaces or between care workers, service users, visitors and families.
- Destroys bacteria.
- Barrier methods reduce or prevent the likely transfer of bacteria.
- Reduces places where bacteria can be trapped.
- Ensures a high standard of hygiene.
- Reduces the opportunities for spreading bacteria.
- Stops others from coming into contact with bacteria, so reducing cross-infection.

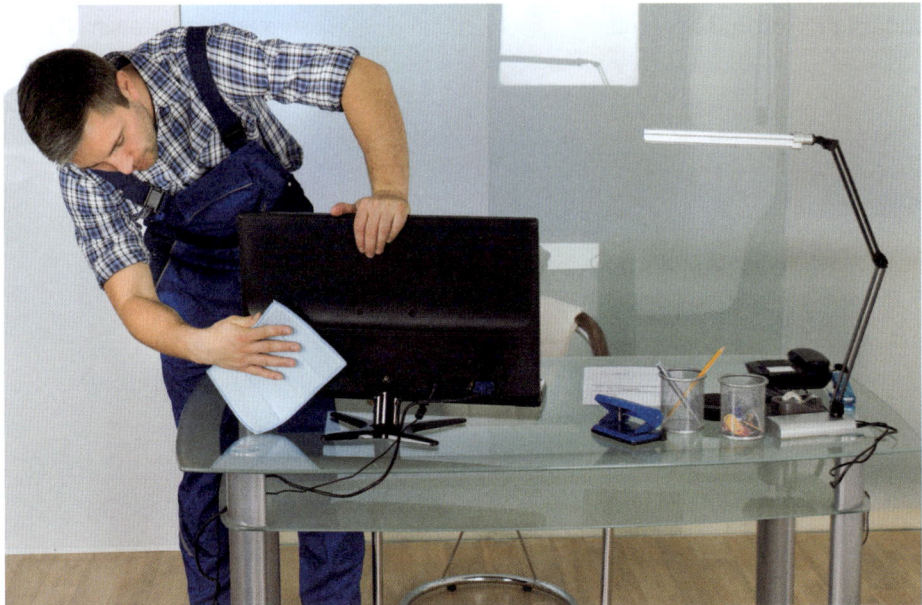

Figure 4.6 All surfaces and equipment need to be cleaned regularly

> **Exam tip**
>
> Always read the question carefully. Often exam questions will be set in the context of a specific care setting.
>
> Check: is the question asking about hygiene in a health or a social care setting? Make sure your answer relates to the correct type of setting.

> **Revision activity**
>
> Produce a spider diagram for each type of care setting (healthcare and social care).
>
> Include as many ways as you can of maintaining good standards of hygiene and cleanliness in each type of setting.

> **Typical mistake**
>
> Giving vague answers will not gain marks. For example, if you are asked how a care worker can maintain high standards of cleanliness in a care setting, stating 'keep everything clean' lacks detail and would not gain marks.
>
> To gain higher marks your answer should include some specific ways of keeping the environment clean, such as vacuuming carpets every day or washing down work surfaces with hot soapy water.

> **Now test yourself**   TESTED
>
> 1. Identify **three** ways a GP surgery could ensure high standards of general cleanliness.
> 2. Look closely at Figure 4.5. Identify and explain the good hygiene practices you can see.
> 3. Describe how a high standard of general cleanliness could be maintained in a day centre.
> 4. Figure 4.6 shows a desk and computer being cleaned. Give reasons why this is important in the following care settings:
>   - on a hospital ward
>   - in the residents' lounge at a retirement home.

Personal hygiene measures

REVISED

There are many opportunities for bacteria to grow and for infection to spread in health and social care environments.

A large number of individuals may use a care setting over the course of a day. Many different activities take place, such as:
- physical examinations at a GP surgery
- treatments given at a hospital
- meals being prepared and served in a day centre or primary school.

To prevent the spread of infection, it is very important that everyone working in a care setting has a high standard of personal hygiene.

Bacteria Tiny, microscopic organisms. Some bacteria can cause infection and disease.

Infection When bacteria (germs) invade the body and cause a disease or illness.

Hygiene Practices that keep you and your surroundings clean in order to prevent illness and the spread of disease.

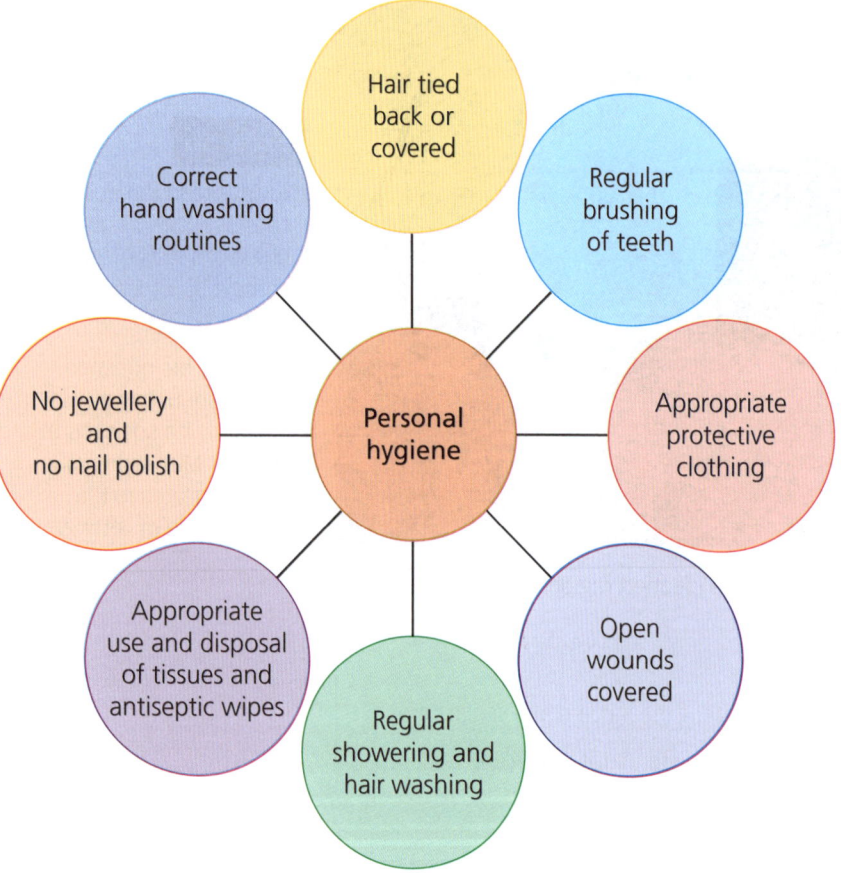

Figure 4.7 Personal hygiene measures for care workers

You can find further details of correct handwashing routines on page 60. Information about the use of appropriate protective clothing in health and social care settings is on pages 61–2.
- Regular showering: individuals who shower morning and evening every day carry fewer bacteria. This will reduce the spread of infection. Showering keeps the body clean; this kills bacteria and prevents body odour.
- Regular hair washing: this keeps the hair clean and will prevent infections such as head lice. If dirty hair comes into contact with patients, it could lead to a spread of infection. So if hair is washed frequently, it reduces opportunities for spreading of bacteria.
- Regular brushing of teeth: this avoids infections such as halitosis that can cause bad breath, which can be unpleasant for individuals being cared for. It reduces levels of bacteria in the mouth.

Exam-style question answers at www.hoddereducation.co.uk/myrevisionnotesdownloads

How good personal hygiene protects individuals

Good personal hygiene ensures a high level of individual cleanliness and helps stop the spread of infection between care workers and service users.

- Good personal hygiene prevents the transfer of bacteria.
- Thorough handwashing removes bacteria, as does use of anti-bacterial hand gel.
- Individuals who have regular showers and clean their hair and teeth carry fewer bacteria, which reduces the risk of spreading infection.
- Barrier methods (protective clothing and wounds covered) help to reduce and prevent the transfer of bacteria (cross-contamination) and spread of infection.
- Jewellery can trap bacteria, so not wearing it removes places for bacteria to be trapped, such as on rings and bracelets.
- Not wearing nail polish prevents contamination as it could chip or flake off into food or into a patient's wound, for example.
- Tying hair back or covering it prevents it from dropping into food and contaminating it with any bacteria that are present.
- Using and disposing of tissues and antiseptic wipes appropriately prevents the spread of infection – this includes covering your mouth and nose with a tissue when sneezing.
    - Antiseptic wipes and hand gel can be a handy way of sterilising the skin to avoid the spread of infection.
    - Special first aid antiseptic wipes are used for cleaning wounds such as minor cuts and scratches.
    - All used wipes and tissues should be disposed of immediately after use in a covered bin.

> **Cross-contamination** When bacteria spread onto food from another source, such as hands, work surfaces, kitchen equipment and utensils, or between cooked and raw food.
>
> **Contamination** When something is tainted with other substances that may be unclean – for example, disease-causing bacteria.

Personal hygiene rules when preparing and serving food

- Wash and dry hands thoroughly before and after touching food.
- Avoid coughing and sneezing near food – use a tissue if you need to cough or sneeze and dispose of it straight away.
- Wash hands immediately after using a tissue before touching any food or utensils.
- Food should not be prepared by anyone who is unwell with diarrhoea, a cough or a cold as bacteria will easily spread onto the food.
- Cuts and scratches should be covered with a coloured waterproof plaster.
- Hair should be tied back or covered with a hairnet or food hygiene hat.
- A clean apron or overall should be worn to prevent bacteria from clothes coming into contact with food.

> **Typical mistake**
>
> Don't mix up personal hygiene with general cleanliness. General cleanliness relates to the environment, whereas personal hygiene relates to the individual.

> **Revision activity**
>
> Learn all of the examples of personal hygiene measures by:
> - making a copy of Figure 4.7, Personal hygiene measures for care workers
> - adding to the diagram by writing a reason why each hygiene measure is important.

> **Now test yourself** — TESTED
>
> 1. Give the meaning of the term 'personal hygiene'.
> 2. Explain why care workers should not wear jewellery or nail polish.
> 3. Explain how good personal hygiene protects service users.
> 4. Explain how good personal hygiene protects care workers.
> 5. List **four** personal hygiene rules for someone working in a care setting.

Hand washing routines

The most common way of spreading bacteria is by the hands. Germs accumulate on the hands as an individual touches surfaces, objects and people throughout the day.

Frequently washing hands limits the transfer of bacteria and viruses and so reduces the chance of spreading infection. The correct technique to use for washing hands is shown in Figure 4.8.

Hand-washing technique with soap and water

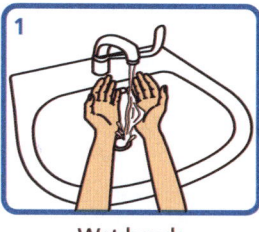
1. Wet hands with water

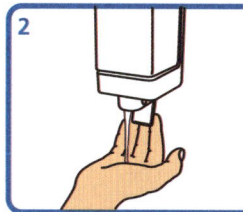
2. Apply enough soap to cover all hand surfaces

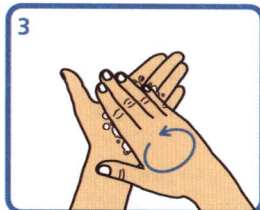
3. Rub hands palm to palm

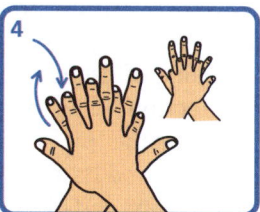
4. Rub back of each hand with palm of other hand with fingers interlaced

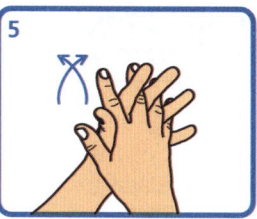
5. Rub palm to palm with fingers interlaced

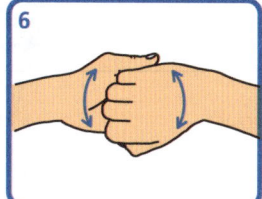
6. Rub with back of fingers to opposing palms with fingers interlocked

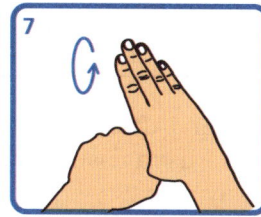
7. Rub each thumb clasped in opposite hand using a rotational movement

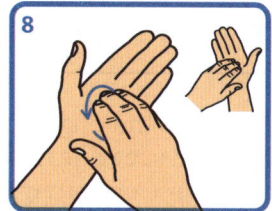
8. Rub tips of fingers in opposite palm in a circular motion

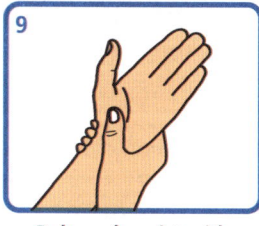
9. Rub each wrist with opposite hand

10. Rinse hands with water

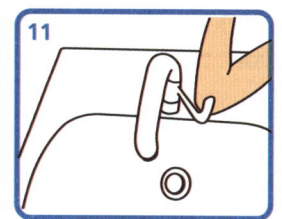
11. Use elbow to turn off tap

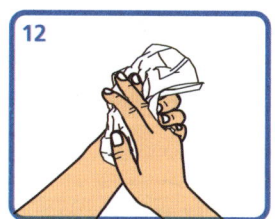
12. Dry thoroughly with a single-use towel

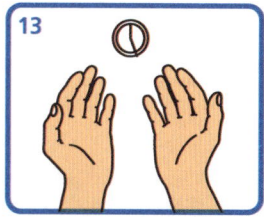
13. Hand washing should take 15–30 seconds

Figure 4.8 Correct hand washing procedure

Note: hands should always be dried thoroughly after washing.

Exam-style question answers at www.hoddereducation.co.uk/myrevisionnotesdownloads

When should care workers wash their hands?

Care workers should always wash their hands:
- before putting on and after removing disposable gloves
- before and after treating wounds or caring for a sick or injured person
- before and after providing personal care for an individual such as feeding them or helping them get dressed
- before and after changing a nappy or incontinence pad
- before and after preparing or handling any food
- after handling clinical waste
- after clearing up rubbish and putting it in the bin
- after clearing up resources such as toys or equipment
- after coughing or using a tissue to blow their nose
- after touching their face or hair
- after using the toilet.

> **Revision activity**
>
> Create a flow chart showing the main stages for thorough hand washing.

> **Typical mistake**
>
> Some students make the mistake of stating that hands should be washed 'after' a certain activity, when they need to be washed before as well.

> **Exam tip**
>
> Make sure that you know examples of when it is essential for care workers to wash their hands, as well as the reasons why it is necessary.

> **Now test yourself** TESTED
>
> 1. Give **four** examples of occasions when care workers should wash their hands.
> 2. Describe the correct routine for washing hands in a way that an individual with learning difficulties can understand.
> 3. Explain why thorough hand washing is very important in care settings.

Personal protective equipment (PPE)   REVISED

Wearing protective clothing and equipment is a barrier method for preventing the spread of infection. The clothing can prevent the transfer of bacteria from a care worker to a service user and vice versa.

Protective clothing is sometimes referred to as PPE, which stands for 'personal protective equipment'.

Appropriate protective clothing is shown in Figure 4.9.

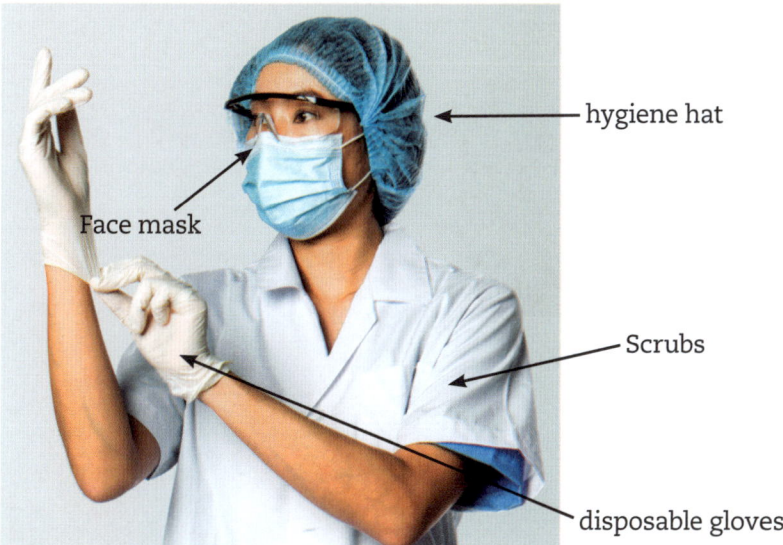

Figure 4.9 Appropriate protective clothing must be used in a healthcare setting

Cambridge National Level 1/2 Health and Social Care

Wearing disposable aprons

A fresh apron should be used for each new task. Examples of when they should be worn are:
- bathing a service user
- changing soiled bed linen
- dressing wounds
- assisting someone with toileting
- putting on cream for someone who has a skin condition such as psoriasis or eczema
- dealing with incontinence pads.

Wearing disposable gloves/rubber gloves

A fresh pair of disposable gloves should be used for each new task. Examples of when they should be worn are:
- changing incontinence pads
- changing soiled bed linen
- dressing wounds
- clearing up spillages, e.g. vomit, blood
- food preparation and serving
- when carrying out general cleaning – rubber gloves.

Wearing face masks

These are effective barriers for retaining droplets that can be released when talking, sneezing or coughing.

Wearing hairnets or hygiene hats

These are particularly important when preparing or serving food. If hair is not tied back or covered it is more likely to fall into food and staff are more likely to touch their hair. This can spread bacteria to food.

Wearing tabards or overalls

Overalls or tabards provide a barrier covering the individual's clothes. This reduces the likelihood of transferring bacteria.

Surgical garments and overshoes

They provide a barrier and reduce the likelihood of contamination during procedures such as surgery or dental work. This barrier protects both the patient and care professional from contact with blood or other bodily fluid that can cause contamination and so reduces the likelihood of transferring bacteria.

> **Exam tip**
>
> Learn examples of protective clothing that could be used by care workers in different types of care settings. Make sure you can give reasons for their use.

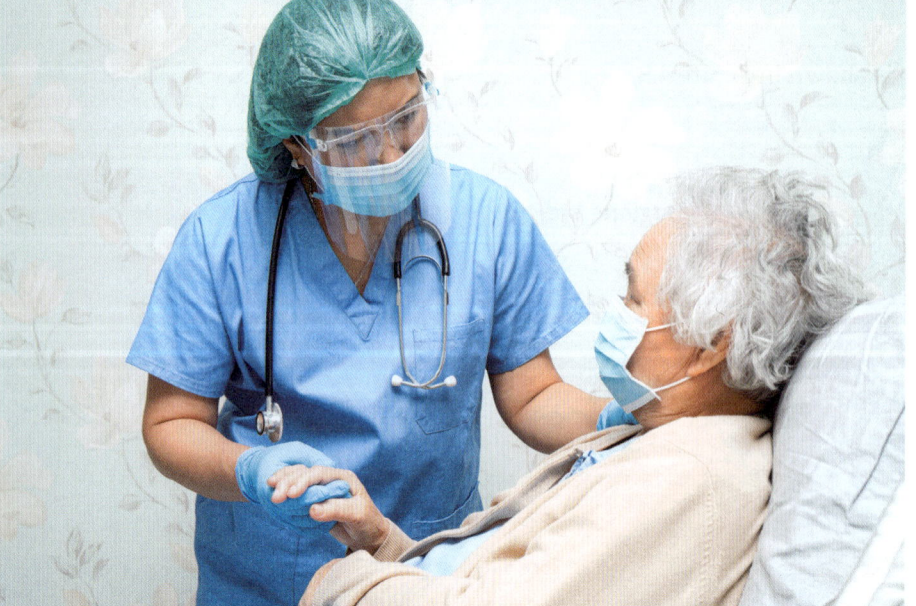

Figure 4.10 What kinds of protective clothing are being used here?

Exam-style question answers at **www.hoddereducation.co.uk/myrevisionnotesdownloads**

> **Revision activity**
>
> Look carefully at Figure 4.10. Identify each piece of protective clothing that is being used. Explain why each one is being used and how it protects the care worker and the service users.

> **Typical mistake**
>
> When identifying an example of protective clothing, do not just state 'gloves' or 'hat'. You need to be specific, for example 'a hygiene hat' or 'rubber gloves'.

Figure 4.11 Serving food at a children's lunch club

> **Now test yourself** — TESTED
>
> 1 Identify **three** examples of protective clothing that could be worn by a care worker changing soiled bed sheets for a care home resident.
> 2 Identify **three** tasks for which a care worker should wear disposable gloves.
> 3 Give reasons why a hygiene hat would be worn.
> 4 When and why would a face mask be worn in a care setting?
> 5 Look closely at Figure 4.11. Identify the protective clothing you can see and explain why it is good hygiene practice in the children's lunch club.

Topic area 4: Protecting service users and service providers in health and social care settings

63

Cambridge National Level 1/2 Health and Social Care

4.3 Safety procedures and measures

Safety procedures

REVISED

- A procedure is a process, not a specific action. It is a set of actions that are carried out in a particular order.
- A procedure informs care workers and service users about what they have to do and how it should be done to ensure everyone's safety.
- Safety procedures are guidelines about how to deal with emergency situations such as fire, or how to arrange a safe trip for care home residents, for example.

Table 4.3 Safety procedures and how they protect individuals

Examples of safety procedures	How individuals are protected
- Emergency evacuation procedure, practised with regular fire drills - 'Run, Hide, Tell' procedure for a terrorist attack	- Ensures staff know their responsibilities in an emergency, enables them to take quick and efficient action - Provides guidance for staff and service users to help keep them safe
- DBS checks for all staff - Safeguarding policy and procedures	- Ensures checks are carried out so staff are safe to work with, for example, children and vulnerable adults, in care settings - Staff are aware of safeguarding issues and what action to take
- First aid policy and procedures	- Appropriate treatment by trained staff
- Food safety policy and procedures	- Promotes good food hygiene practice - Reduces the risk of food poisoning
- Risk assessments for activities, outings and trips, equipment	- Individuals are protected from avoidable injuries - Equipment will be fit for purpose, no worn-out or damaged equipment will be in use
- Complying with the requirements of legislation – such as the Health and Safety at Work Act	- Promotes good practice - Ensures a safe environment for individuals in the care setting
- Staff training – safeguarding, manual handling, first aid, etc.	- Alerts staff to potential dangers - Enables staff to do their job safely - Reduces risks and ensures a safer environment
- Ensuring an appropriate staff to child ratio (or resident or patient, etc.)	- The level of supervision will be related to individual needs - Improves the standard of care and safety levels

Safety measures

REVISED

A safety measure is a specific action such as putting up a fire safety notice or using a 'wet floor' sign after mopping the floor.

Table 4.4 Safety measures and how they protect individuals

Examples of safety measures	How individuals are protected
<ul><li>Fire safety notices in every room in the care setting</li><li>Signs indicating fire exits and assembly points</li><li>Fire doors kept clear</li><li>A fire extinguisher available by each external exit</li><li>A fire blanket available in kitchen areas</li><li>Fire alarms throughout the building</li></ul>	<ul><li>Promotes awareness of safety procedures</li><li>Informs care workers and service users of where to go and what to do in an emergency</li><li>Helps to keep staff and service users safe</li></ul>
<ul><li>Safety warning signs such as 'wet floor', 'no smoking', 'corrosive', 'no entry'</li></ul>	<ul><li>Raises individuals' awareness of possible hazards</li><li>Prevents accidents</li></ul>
<ul><li>Wearing protective clothing</li></ul>	<ul><li>Wearing items such as goggles prevents injury</li><li>Aprons, disposable gloves, etc. help prevent the spread of infection</li></ul>

> **Exam tip**
>
> Make sure that you know examples of safety 'measures' and safety 'procedures'. Make sure that you can explain how they protect care workers and service users.

Figure 4.12 A wet floor sign is a safety measure

> **Typical mistake**
>
> Avoid mixing up 'safety measures' with 'safety procedures'. Make sure that you know the difference. Remember:
> - a procedure is a process that is followed, such as a fire drill
> - a measure is a particular action such as putting up a 'wet floor' sign.

> **Revision activity**
>
> Produce two concept maps, one for safety measures, the other for safety procedures. Include examples of how they protect individuals.

Topic area 4: Protecting service users and service providers in health and social care settings

Cambridge National Level 1/2 Health and Social Care

> **Now test yourself** TESTED
>
> 1. Explain the difference between a safety 'measure' and a safety 'procedure'.
> 2. Describe **four** ways day centre staff could ensure a safe environment for the teenagers attending.
> 3. What are DBS checks?
> 4. Give **three** benefits of having regular fire drills in a care setting.
> 5. State **two** benefits of providing staff with training in safety procedures.

Procedures for reducing risks and promoting good practice

REVISED

Accident prevention

The most common types of accidents in any workplace are slips, trips and falls. Figure 4.13 shows some ways to avoid this type of accident.

Figure 4.13 Ways of preventing slips, trips and falls in care settings

The second most common type of accident is muscle strains from manual handling. This type of injury can be avoided if staff are trained to carry out their manual handling tasks correctly.

Different types of care setting have potentially different types of accidents. For example, the likelihood of a sharps injury is higher in a hospital than in a day centre.

Sharps injury When the skin is punctured by a needle or blade, such as a scalpel, or other medical instrument.

Exam-style question answers at www.hoddereducation.co.uk/myrevisionnotesdownloads

Staff training

One of the best ways to minimise the risk of accidents and to promote good practice is to train staff. Training raises awareness and develops knowledge and skills. The staff will then know:
- the procedures to prevent accidents in the care setting
- the policies they have to follow
- their specific roles and responsibilities.

Training enables staff to:
- develop the skills and knowledge to avoid injuries to themselves and service users
- gain awareness of security measures used to keep individuals safe
- understand how to apply the values of care
- develop knowledge of effective communication
- carry out first aid
- understand safeguarding procedures
- have knowledge of health and safety policies and procedures
- carry out risk assessments
- carry out moving and handling techniques safely.

Policies

All health and social care settings have policies in place. A policy is a plan which outlines:
- the purpose of the policy
- the instructions to achieve the policy's aim of keeping service users safe and promoting their rights.

Policies also ensure that the care setting is complying with the requirements of legislation. Examples of policies found in care settings include:
- accident reporting
- bullying
- confidentiality
- equal opportunities
- fire evacuation
- first aid
- health and safety
- manual handling
- medicines administration records
- risk assessment
- safeguarding.

Risk assessment

The aim of carrying out risk assessment procedures is to identify potential hazards to the health, safety and security of care workers, service users and visitors to a care setting.

Some activities, equipment and care provided in care settings can present hazards. A risk assessment is used to identify ways that these hazards can be minimised or removed completely.

> **Risk** The likelihood that someone or something could be harmed.
>
> **Hazard** Anything that could cause harm, e.g. a faulty piece of equipment or a particular activity.
>
> **Risk assessment** The process of evaluating the likelihood of a hazard actually causing harm.

> **Revision activity**
>
> To help you remember ways to prevent accidents and promote good practice use these three headings:
> - Information
> - Guidelines
> - Procedures.
>
> For example:
> - **P**rocedures: fire drill, evacuation plan, risk assessment, accident procedure.
> - **I**nformation: escape route map in case of fire, wet floor sign, fire exit sign, staff training.
> - **G**uidelines: manual handling policy, health and safety policy, reporting accidents.

> **Exam tip**
>
> Make sure you know examples of procedures, information and guidelines that help prevent accidents and promote good practice.

> **Now test yourself** **TESTED**
>
> 1. Name **two** procedures that should be followed in a care setting.
> 2. State the benefits to care workers of following the two procedures you named in question 1.
> 3. Describe **three** benefits of providing staff with training.
> 4. Identify **three** policies that should be in place in a care setting.

Risk assessments

REVISED

The purpose of carrying out risk assessments is to:
- check that equipment is safe and fit for purpose
- check what could cause harm to people using the care setting
- ensure that the care setting building itself is safe
- identify potential dangers, e.g. trip hazards, risky activities
- prevent accidents, illness and danger
- work out what could go wrong with an activity
- assess how much supervision is needed
- identify ways of controlling and minimising hazards
- ensure any planned trips or visits are safe to proceed.

Risk assessments must be carried out because:
- it is a legal requirement under the Health and Safety at Work Act. Keeping a written record provides evidence that the risk assessments have been carried out
- staff, service users and visitors have a right to be protected and kept safe from harm
- staff, service users and visitors will feel confident using the service knowing that risk assessments are carried out.

Table 4.5 Carrying out a risk assessment involves five steps

Risk assessment	
Step 1	Look for hazards associated with the activity.
Step 2	Identify who might be harmed and how.
Step 3	Consider the level of risk – decide on the precautions or control measures needed to reduce the risk.
Step 4	Make a written record of the findings.
Step 5	Review the risk assessment regularly and improve precautions or control measures if necessary.

> **Control measures** Actions that can be taken to reduce the risks posed by a hazard or to remove the hazard altogether.

Types of hazards in care settings

As with any environment, a care setting could have many hazards, including:
- trip hazards such as rugs, trailing cables, toys or other objects on the floor, or wet floors
- blocked fire exits
- lack of security
- unsafe storage of hazardous substances, e.g. cleaning materials, chemicals, medication
- inadequate supervision
- unsafe, faulty or worn-out equipment
- unsafe soft furnishings or furniture.

The importance of risk assessments

- As already stated, risk assessment is a legal requirement. In settings with more than five employees, risk assessments must be recorded.
- The purpose is to reduce the risk of harm to service users, visitors and staff.

Exam-style question answers at www.hoddereducation.co.uk/myrevisionnotesdownloads

- Staff must identify potential hazards, for example in a day centre, nursing home or hospital ward (e.g. by taking a walk around the setting looking for things that may cause harm to patients, small children or staff, such as faulty electrical equipment).
- Staff must identify potential hazards that may occur during planned activities or outings with adults and children (e.g. using scissors for cutting out with inadequate staff supervision, lack of wheelchair access, trip hazards).
- When potential hazards in the setting are identified, action must be taken so that accidents and harm are avoided.

Willowfield Residential Home				
Activity	Hazards identified	Control measures required	Level of risk	Date for review
Transferring Mrs Smith from her wheelchair into the bath	Broken hoist. Possible lifting injuries – bruising, muscle strain or worse	Equipment log book to record any damage to equipment – to be checked daily. Maintenance book to ensure that equipment is regularly checked	High	Weekly
Fire drill	Wheelchairs stored in front of fire doors – delaying access to fire door	Arrange for wheelchair storage away from the fire exit. Use of folding wheelchairs for safer storage	High	Weekly
Residents' art class	Spillages – water and paint on the floor trip hazard – risk of falls causing sprains, bruising, broken limbs	Supervision – one additional member of staff to assist residents. Cleaner available during the class to mop up spills straightaway	Medium	At each class

Figure 4.14 Example risk assessment for Willowfield Residential home

Revision activity

Make a blank copy of the table in Figure 4.14 (just add the column headings). Then carry out a risk assessment for each of the following:
- a cutting and sticking activity in a day centre
- vacuuming the residents' lounge in a retirement home
- giving medication to a hospital patient.

Now test yourself

TESTED

1. What is the difference between a hazard and a risk?
2. What is a 'control measure'?
3. Explain the purpose of each of the five stages of a risk assessment.
4. Identify **three** possible hazards in the lounge area of a retirement home.

Exam tip

Be able to:
- describe the purpose of carrying out risk assessments
- identify hazards in care settings
- explain ways of reducing the risks (control measures).

Typical mistake

Don't mix up 'risk' and 'hazard'. Be clear about the difference.

Moving and handling techniques

REVISED

Care workers often have to move items of equipment – trolleys, boxes, tables and chairs – and sometimes they have to physically help individuals to move.

It is essential that anyone who has to move or handle as part of their role is trained to do this properly. Individuals receiving care, or care workers themselves, may be injured if they attempt manual handling incorrectly.

The Manual Handling Operations Regulations (1992) define 'manual handling' as 'any transporting of a load including lifting, putting down, pushing, pulling, carrying or moving' of the load.

A load can be a person or an object.

Situations when moving and handling might be necessary

- Transferring a patient from a hospital bed to a chair.
- Assisting an elderly person with their mobility, for example helping them to get out of a chair or into a bath or shower.
- Arranging tables and chairs in a day centre.
- Carrying boxes of toys or books.
- Pushing trolleys, drip stands, wheelchairs, etc.
- Moving a commode into an elderly person's bedroom.
- A home care assistant carrying shopping bags.

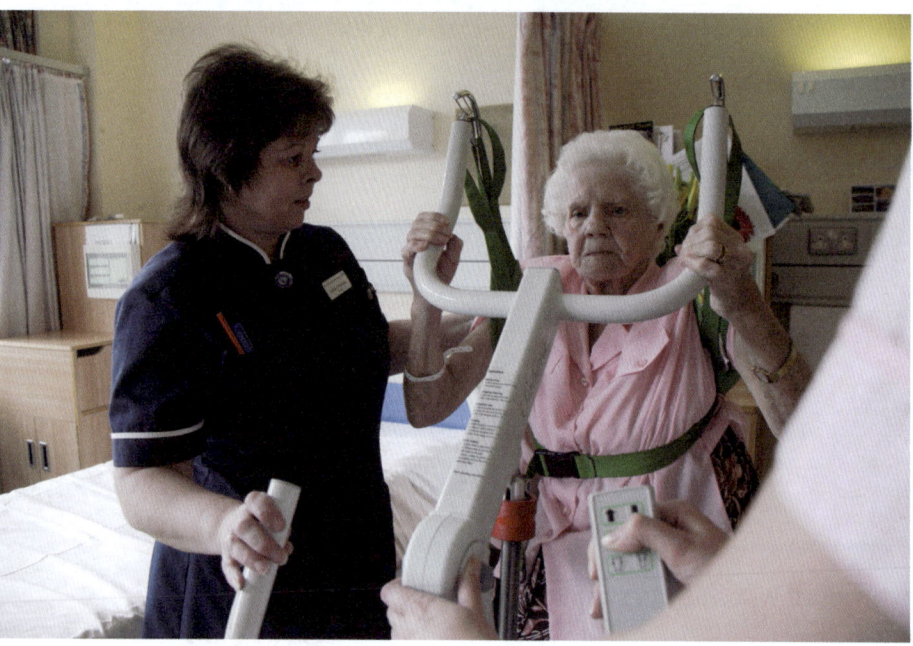

Figure 4.15 This nurse will have been given training in how to use this hoist safely to move a patient

Moving people

It is important to use effective communication skills to tell the person what you are going to do in a way that they will understand. Always ask the person for their permission to carry out the move.

When moving people:
- bend your knees not your back
- avoid twisting your back as this can cause damage to the spine
- use the specialist equipment provided (as long as you have been trained to use it).

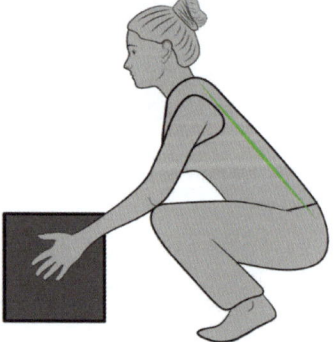
correct posture

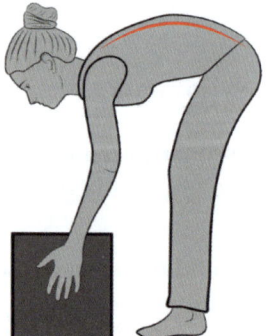
incorrect posture

Figure 4.16 Always use the safe-lifting posture to avoid injury

Exam-style question answers at www.hoddereducation.co.uk/myrevisionnotesdownloads

Moving objects

- Only move objects if really necessary.
- Only lift as much as you can carry easily – do not lift as much as you can, this can cause injury.
- Check that there are no dangers in the environment such as an uneven or slippery floor and that there is enough space to carry out the move.
- Bend your knees, avoid twisting the back or moving sideways.
- Keep feet wide apart for stability.
- Hold the item being lifted close to your body.
- Move smoothly, not jerkily – this reduces the risk of injury.
- Use appropriate equipment, such as a trolley or a box on wheels.
- Shopping should be split between two bags and carried one in each hand to spread the load.

Safe manual handling

- Always check whether the move or lift is really necessary – do not carry out a move unless it is unavoidable.
- Identify any risks involved in carrying out the move and take steps to avoid or minimise risks identified.
- Use a lifting aid if appropriate rather than carry out the lift yourself.
- If the move has been assessed to require two people, do not attempt the move on your own.
- Only ever carry out manual handling if you have been trained to do so.

How correct moving and handling techniques protect individuals

- Manual handling training provides staff with guidance on good practice so they will know how to lift and move individuals safely – this gives them more confidence.
- Risks to service users and staff will be assessed and minimised.
- Staff will know if a second person is needed for the manual handling task.
- Staff will do their job correctly – this ensures a safer environment.
- Service users will have more confidence in staff who have been trained in manual handling – this will help them relax when being moved because they trust the staff.
- Prevents injuries to both service users and care workers.
- Being trained protects staff from accusations of abuse as correct techniques will be used so service users will feel comfortable and will be treated with dignity and respect.

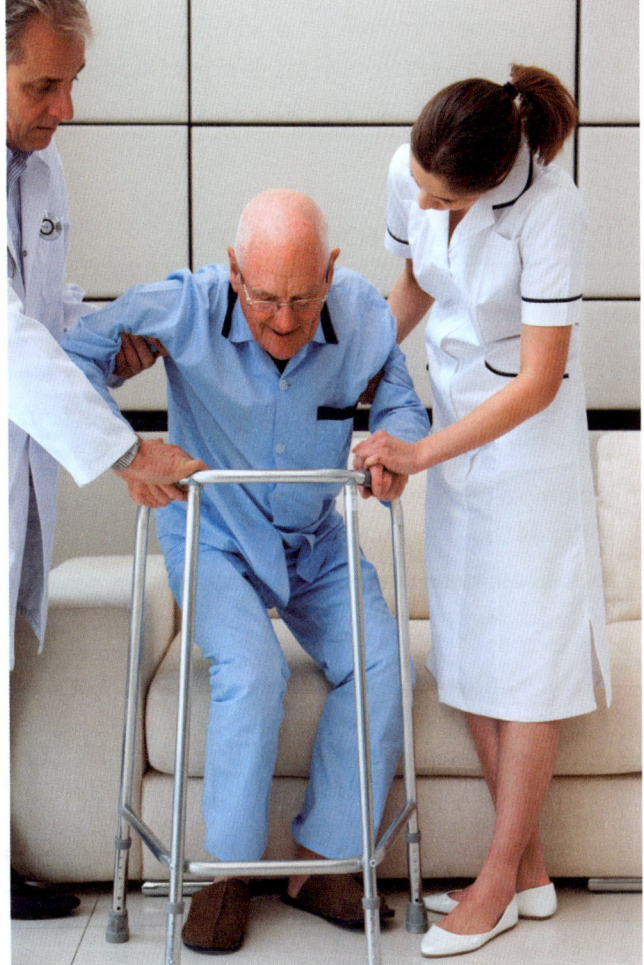

Figure 4.17 Moving and handling individuals often requires two people

> **Exam tip**
>
> Be able to give examples of correct moving and handling techniques and how these protect care workers and service users.

> **Typical mistake**
>
> Some candidates forget to mention that moving and handling must be risk assessed and that two people, who are both trained, are often needed to carry out the move.

> **Revision activity**
>
> Produce an information sheet for a care assistant in a residential care home, with key instructions about moving people safely.

> **Now test yourself** TESTED
>
> 1 Identify **four** situations when moving and handling might be necessary.
> 2 Why is it important to use effective communication skills to explain to an individual that they are going to be moved in a hoist like the one in Figure 4.15?
> 3 Describe the correct procedure and posture for safely moving a box of toys.
> 4 State **three** ways of ensuring safe manual handling.
> 5 State **three** ways care workers are protected by using correct manual handling techniques.

Emergency procedures REVISED

Emergency procedures in care settings include fire drills and evacuations.

Fire procedures

Every care setting must have a fire emergency evacuation plan. This will include the action to be taken by all staff in the event of a fire.

An example of an evacuation procedure for a nursing home is shown in Figure 4.18.

Checkleigh Nursing Home
Fire evacuation procedure

- If you discover a fire, raise the alarm – alert people in the immediate area, activate alarm system, call 999.
- All staff to remove people from their immediate area – direct them to the fire assembly point, use designated fire exits, never use lifts.
- Designated staff assist residents with:
  - mobility difficulties (use of evac chairs/wheelchairs)
  - hearing difficulties (may not hear alarm)
  - dementia patients (may be confused/unaware of what is happening).
- Staff to close doors and windows, switch off lights as they leave.
- Staff evacuating the building must check their locality is clear.
- Everyone to assemble at designated external assembly point to await further instructions.
- Do not re-enter the building until told it is safe to do so.
- Carry out head count to ensure everyone is accounted for.
- Senior staff to inform fire brigade if anyone is left in the building.

Figure 4.18 Example of a nursing home fire evacuation procedure

Exam-style question answers at www.hoddereducation.co.uk/myrevisionnotesdownloads

Fire safety measures include:
- fire safety notices throughout the care setting
- signs indicating fire exits
- signs indicating assembly points
- a fire extinguisher by each exit
- a fire blanket in kitchen areas.

Fire drills should be practised regularly – at least once a year – so that staff and service users are fully aware of the procedures to follow. New staff should be trained when they start work.

Evacuation procedures

Emergency events, such as a:
- gas leak
- flood
- bomb threat

will require a setting to be evacuated quickly and efficiently to keep people safe.

In the very rare event of a firearms or weapons attack, the government has provided advice on how individuals can keep themselves safe. Leaflets, posters and YouTube films are available.

You are advised to:
- Run – if you can.
- Hide – if you can't run away.
- Tell – the police when it is safe to do so.

Care settings are encouraged to ensure that they raise awareness of this advice sensitively, particularly with children.

Figure 4.19 'Stay safe' advice

First aid

In case of health emergencies, care settings must have enough trained first aiders available for the number of staff and service users.

The health needs of the service users would also be taken into account. For example, a residential home would need more first aiders than a dentist's surgery due to the number of residents and their overall state of health.

First aiders must:
- be trained
- be up to date in their knowledge.

Some staff should be trained to use an Epipen, based on an assessment of the number of individuals in a care setting who are at risk of anaphylactic shock.

All care settings must have a first aid policy.

How emergency procedures protect individuals

- They ensure that everyone is kept as safe as possible and away from danger.
- They ensure the care setting complies with health and safety legislation.
- They provide guidance for staff so that they know exactly what to do in an emergency.
- They enable staff to take quick and efficient action to remove service users and themselves from danger.
- They provide guidance for service users so that they know what to do in an emergency.
- Individuals using services will be reassured by knowing these procedures exist to help them in an emergency.
- Awareness that staff are trained to deal with emergency situations reduces anxiety for service users and instils trust.

> **Epipen** An emergency treatment for someone with a severe anaphylactic reaction. It is an automatic injector device which contains a dose of the hormone adrenaline, which is injected into the thigh.
>
> **Anaphylactic shock** An extreme allergic reaction. Common causes can be nuts, celery, seafood, and wasp or bee stings.

> **Exam tip**
>
> Make sure you can give specific examples of emergency procedures and the reasons why they protect care workers and service users.

> **Typical mistake**
>
> Don't mix up 'fire procedures' and 'fire safety measures'. Make sure you know the difference.

> **Revision activity**
>
> Read the nursing home fire evacuation procedure, shown in Figure 4.18. For each of the bullet points, explain how the action described protects individuals.

> **Now test yourself** TESTED
>
> 1. List **four** points that should be included in a care setting fire evacuation procedure.
> 2. Discuss how the fire evacuation procedure shown in Figure 4.18 benefits both service users and service providers.
> 3. State **four** fire safety measures that a day centre should have in place to protect individuals using the care setting.
> 4. How would a care setting work out the number of trained first aiders they need?

Equipment considerations REVISED

Care workers in health and social care settings will use a range of equipment with service users, ranging from mobility aids and manual handling equipment to toys and household appliances.

Staff should be appropriately trained to use specialist equipment such as:
- hoists
- transfer boards
- slings
- slide sheets
- leg-lifters
- fire evacuation chairs.

Equipment safety

- Use of equipment should be risk assessed to ensure it is safe and fit for purpose and that the staff are trained to use it safely.
- Equipment and toys for use with children should be checked for small or loose components that could be choking hazards.
- For younger children toys should be age appropriate. Most toys have an age advice label.
- The BSI Kitemark™ symbol confirms that the item has been tested by the British Standards Institution and that it meets the required safety standards.
- All equipment and toys in care settings should have appropriate safety labels. Examples of safety labels are shown in Figure 4.20.

Figure 4.20 The BSI Kitemark™, Lion Mark and age advice safety symbols

Equipment should be fit for purpose

- Equipment should be appropriate for the task being carried out and in good condition.
- Specialist equipment should be available if needed, for example to assist individuals to move from a wheelchair into a bath.
- Equipment should be maintained in good working order, for example hoists serviced regularly.
- Care settings should have a reporting system for damaged or faulty equipment so that it can either be repaired or disposed of.
- Care settings should have a replacement programme for older or worn-out equipment.

Regular maintenance checks

Regular maintenance checks should be carried out to ensure:
- faults are spotted early
- repairs are carried out as soon as they are needed
- any damaged items, such as toys, wheelchairs, safety gates and so on, are disposed of or repaired as appropriate
- electrical equipment is PAT tested annually and taken out of use if not safe.

How equipment considerations improve safety

- Damage is spotted early before anyone is injured.
- Correct equipment is provided for the task.
- Staff are trained and so know how to use the equipment correctly – this prevents injuries to themselves or to the service users.
- Specialist equipment is available when needed, for example hoists, fire evacuation chairs, etc., so that service users are handled safely.
- Electrical equipment is safe so the risk of injury is reduced.
- Ensures the care setting is complying with health and safety legislation.

> **Exam tip**
>
> Make sure that you can explain how equipment considerations improve safety in care settings. Be able to give examples to develop your explanation.

> **Revision activity**
>
> Make a list of equipment used by a day centre for children with physical disabilities. Write an explanation of the equipment considerations that should be in place so that a safe standard of care is provided.
>
> Repeat this for:
> - a retirement home
> - a GP surgery.

> **Typical mistake**
>
> Students sometimes give answers relating only to specialist equipment in care settings, such as hoists. They forget to include everyday items such as televisions, toasters and hairdryers that would be in use in a residential care home for example, or scissors and toys used for example by a support group.

> **Now test yourself** TESTED
>
> 1. How could a community centre manager ensure that toys purchased for use in the centre are safe?
> 2. Explain how having a reporting system for damaged or faulty equipment could help protect care workers and service users.
> 3. What is PAT testing?
> 4. Outline how equipment considerations improve safety in care settings.

Exam-style question answers at www.hoddereducation.co.uk/myrevisionnotesdownloads

4.4 How security measures protect service users and staff

Security measures in health and social care settings are necessary to keep staff and service users safe, for example by stopping unauthorised individuals from entering the care setting.

They are also necessary to prevent vulnerable individuals such as children, or adults with dementia, from leaving the care setting unsupervised.

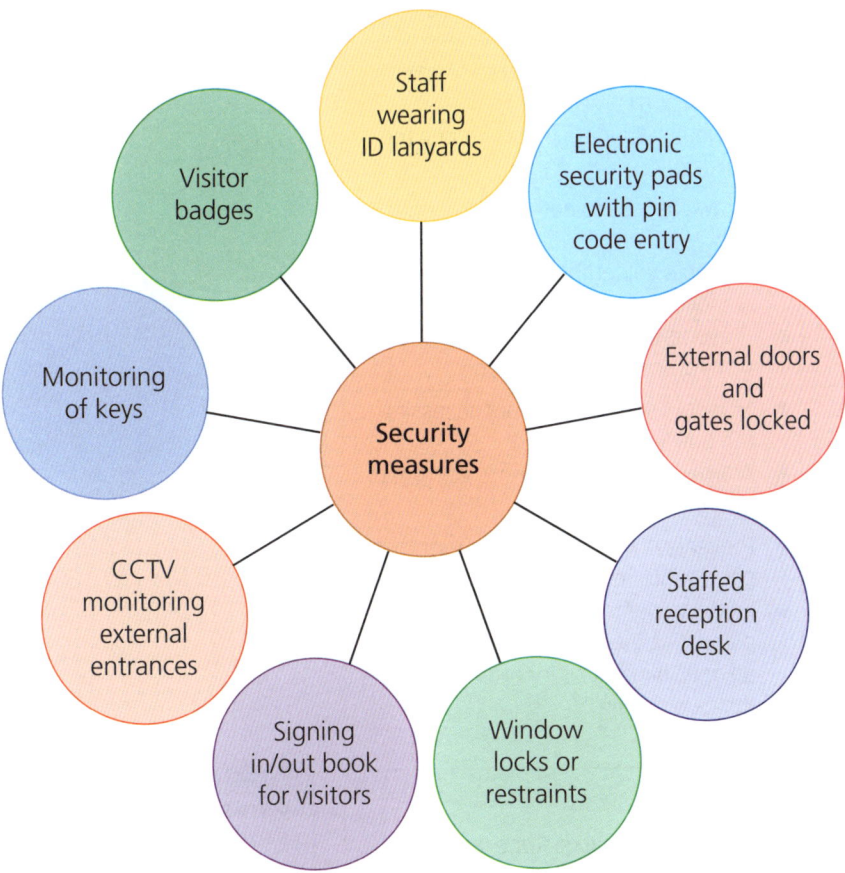

Figure 4.21 Examples of security measures in care settings

How security measures protect individuals

REVISED

Table 4.6 Security of people

Examples of security measures	How individuals are protected
• Staff on duty at the reception desk • Signing in and out book for visitors • Escorting visitors	• Individuals are registered before being allowed into the setting – this identifies who they are. • Controls access to the setting – only authorised people allowed in. • Staff know who is in the care setting and why they are there and where they are at all times. • If the care setting is for children, they will only be released to authorised people, e.g. with a password.
• Issuing visitor badges • Staff wearing ID lanyards • Staff uniform	• Easy to spot unauthorised people as lanyards and/or uniforms quickly identify staff. • Easy to identify visitors.
• Reporting of concerns to managers	• Raises management awareness of security breaches. • Appropriate action can be initiated by senior staff to address security issues.

Cambridge National Level 1/2 Health and Social Care

Table 4.7 Security of the building

Examples of security measures	How individuals are protected
• Having a staff member with responsibility for monitoring and checking external entrances • Having a member of staff on duty at the reception desk	• Controls access to the building. • Only allows authorised individuals to enter the care setting. • Prevents residents, patients, toddlers or children from wandering out of the care setting.
• Locks on external doors • Monitoring of keys	• Only a limited number of people will have keys so access is controlled. • Having a list of 'key holders' ensures the whereabouts of all sets of keys is known at all times. • Prevents intruders from entering the building.
• Security pads with pin codes • Electronic swipe card entry system • Buzzer entry system	• Allows access to authorised people only. • Prevents vulnerable service users from wandering out of the care setting. • Prevents strangers and intruders from gaining access to the setting.
• CCTV monitoring exits and entrances • Alarms on external doors that are not in regular use	• Monitors staff and visitors accessing the building. • Alarms identify if anyone is going in or out unannounced.
• Window locks and window restraints	• Prevents unwanted visitors from getting into the setting. • Keeps vulnerable individuals safe by preventing them from falling through an open window or for example leaving the care setting.

Exam tip

Give precise examples of security measures to achieve more marks. For example, state:
- 'Have a staffed reception desk' not 'Have a reception desk'.
- 'Have a signing in and out book for visitors' not 'Have a logbook'.
- 'Have CCTV cameras to monitor the main external doors' not 'Have cameras in all the rooms'.

Revision activity

Learn all the examples of security measures by making a copy of Figure 4.21 and then extending it by writing an explanation of how each measure protects individuals in care settings.

Typical mistake

Don't give vague explanations of security measures, for example 'all doors should be locked in a care setting to keep people safe'. This would not be appropriate as it is not acceptable to lock individuals into rooms in a care setting.

You could state that all external doors should be locked and have a buzzer so that visitors only gain access through the receptionist. Or you could state that the main entrance should have electronic key pad access to prevent unauthorised access.

Now test yourself TESTED

1. List the benefits of wearing staff lanyards and using visitor badges in a care setting.
2. State **four** ways the staff at a nursing home could ensure that the building is secure.
3. Give **four** ways the staff of a residential care home for adults with dementia could ensure security for the residents.
4. How does monitoring keys help to provide security in a care setting?

Exam-style question answers at www.hoddereducation.co.uk/myrevisionnotesdownloads

Exam-style questions

1. **a** Describe the role of a Designated Safeguarding Lead (DSL). [2]
   b State the purpose of DBS checks. [1]

2. Kai is a dental technician working in a dentist's surgery. He prepares the treatment rooms for use and ensures high standards of hygiene are maintained.

   Identify and explain **two** ways that Kai can help to prevent the spread of infection. Use the headings below and give a different way for each:
   - General cleanliness
   - Appropriate protective clothing [4]

3. Steph works in a care home for elderly people. The care home has recently run a training session for staff about personal hygiene.

   Explain why Steph will have to follow the personal hygiene rules 'no jewellery to be worn' and 'use correct hand washing routines'. [6]

4. Carrying out risk assessments in care settings is an important method of reducing risks and dangers.

   State **two** different activities where risk assessments should be carried out in each of the following types of care settings:
   - A nursing home
   - A community centre running activity sessions for 10-16 year olds [4]

5. Adams House Day Centre runs activities for different groups of people – art classes, book club, yoga and chess, for example. Tea, coffee and a hot lunch are provided. A number of accidents have recently happened at the day centre, such as trips and falls, as well as burns in the kitchen. There have also been two cases of food poisoning.

   Identify **three** safety measures that a health and safety manager at Adams House Day Centre could introduce and describe how each measure could improve the standard of care. [9]

6. Evaluate how providing care home staff with training in manual handling techniques helps to prevent accidents and promotes good practice. [8]

7. Complete the table below to identify which of the examples are safety procedures and which are safety measures. [6]

Example	Safety procedure ✓	Safety measure ✓
Putting up notices in every room explaining what to do in the event of a fire		
Having regular fire drills		
No entry sign to prevent unauthorised access		
Checking for damaged or worn floor coverings		
Putting a 'wet floor' notice in a corridor after it has been mopped		
Carrying out risk assessments		

8. Outline how monitoring of keys is an important security measure in a care setting. [3]

9. Receiving and monitoring visitors is a security measure in place at the local social services department. Explain how this security measure can protect individuals using social services and those who work there. [3]

10. Complete the table with one example of PPE (personal protective equipment) that would be worn by each individual listed. Use a different example for each individual. [3]

Individual	Example of PPE that would be worn
A catering assistant serving lunch at a day centre	
A GP carrying out an examination of a patient	
A care assistant helping an individual to have a shower	

Cambridge National Level 1/2 Health and Social Care

Now test yourself answers

Topic area 1: The rights of service users in health and social care settings

1.1 Types of care settings (page 11)

1 Care or treatment provided in an individual's home.
2 Four types of care:
   - medical care
   - preventative screening, such as blood pressure or glucose monitoring, weight
   - treatment for illness
   - treatment for disease
   - managing disability
   - treating injuries.
3 Two from:
   - homeless shelter
   - day centre
   - foodbank
   - community centre
   - social services department
   - residential care home
   - support group
   - retirement home.

   Types of care:
   - domiciliary care
   - support for those in need – food, somewhere to live
   - practical support, such as shopping, showering, getting dressed, preparing a meal
   - support with mental health.
4 Four from:
   - getting out of bed
   - having a shower
   - getting dressed
   - preparing breakfast
   - cleaning the house
   - going shopping
   - meeting friends.
5 Settings include:
   - ambulance service
   - hospital
   - physiotherapist
   - GP surgery
   - occupational therapist
   - counselling services
   - social services department.

1.2 The rights of service users

The rights of individuals (page 12)

1 Four from:
   - adults
   - babies
   - children
   - young people
   - older adults.
2 By law.
3 All five are required:
   - choice
   - confidentiality
   - consultation
   - protection from abuse and harm
   - equal and fair treatment.

Choice (page 13)

1 Having the opportunity to decide or pick between two or more options.
2 Two from:
   - offered choice of activities/trips/TV programmes/games
   - choice of who to sit with
   - choice of clothes
   - choice of meals/drinks.
3 Two from:
   - menu choices for meals: vegetarian, Halal, Kosher, gluten free, etc.
   - ask what they would like to drink – tea, coffee, water
   - ask if they would like to get up and sit in a chair/go to patients' lounge
   - whether or not they want to see visitors
   - discuss options for treatment
   - male or female nurse/doctor.
4 Answers could include:
   - offering choice of GP
   - male/female GP
   - time of appointment
   - virtual appointment/telephone appointment
   - face-to-face appointment.

Confidentiality (page 15)

1 Limits access to or places restrictions on sharing certain types of sensitive information so that it is kept private to only those who need to be aware of it.
2 Example answers:
   - If the social worker regularly notices unexplained bruising on a baby whose family she visits, the family GP would be informed

Exam-style question answers at www.hoddereducation.co.uk/myrevisionnotesdownloads

so that he or she could check on the baby. The social services safeguarding procedures would also be followed.
- If a vulnerable adult tells the social worker that her son keeps taking money from her purse without asking and she is now worried about paying her bills, but she doesn't want to 'make a fuss about it', the social worker would have to pass this information on to the care team as the son is financially abusing his mother.

3 Two from:
- when someone intends to harm themselves, for example if they say they are going to take their own life
- an individual is threatening to cause harm, for example to beat someone up
- when someone has given information that suggests they are at risk of harm from others, for example child sex abuse
- if an individual has confided that they are involved in dealing drugs.

4 Issues include:
- Care workers often receive very sensitive and private information from service users.
- Service users may be vulnerable and very trusting of those caring for them.
- It is unprofessional to talk about confidential matters outside of the care environment.
- It protects the interests of any individual.
- It helps service users to trust their carers.

Consultation (page 17)

1 The process of discussing something with someone in order to get their advice or opinion so that a decision can be made that is acceptable to all involved.

2 Four from:
- ask for opinions and views
- shared decision-making
- preferences and options
- wants and needs
- likes and dislikes.

3 Two from:
- asking for and listening to their views and opinions
- explaining options
- providing information
- sharing decision-making.

4 Explanation could include:
- asking what type of care they would like if it were possible
- giving information about the options available for treatment of their condition
- explaining what different treatment options will involve – surgery, medication, tests, etc.
- explaining benefits and disadvantages of the different treatments, such as side effects and recovery time
- listening to their views, opinions and preferences for the types of treatment available

- making a shared decision based on opinions given by the individual.

Equal and fair treatment (page 18)

1 Equal treatment means being given the same opportunities and choices as everyone else.
Fair treatment means being able to have full access to those opportunities and choices.

2 Enables all individuals who use wheelchairs or other mobility aids to access the college just like everyone else. Could be staff, visitors, children, their siblings and parents.

3 Ensures that they receive person-centred care that meets their individual needs.

Protection from abuse and harm (page 20)

1 Four from:
- all staff are DBS checked (Disclosure and Barring Service)
- reporting procedures for abusive behaviour
- a designated (child) protection officer is appointed
- complaints procedures
- manual handling training for staff
- safeguarding training for staff
- first aid trained staff available
- fire procedures and fire drills
- emergency evacuation procedures
- lockdown procedure
- risk assessments of equipment and activities
- Health and Safety at Work Act implemented
- policies in place, e.g. confidentiality, 'no secrets', equal opportunities
- high standards of hygiene in the care setting
- security measures in place.

2 Three from:
- an individual lacking mental capacity – they may not be able to tell someone what is happening and may depend on others for care and to make decisions for them
- an individual with dementia – they may not realise that abuse is happening, may have difficulty remembering and communicating
- an individual with a learning disability – they may not know what abuse is or understand their rights
- children in care – children may move in and out of different settings and so not have a trusted adult and they may not know their rights or they may be scared of complaining
- an individual who is visually/hearing impaired – they may be dependent on others for their care and so are less likely to report abuse.

3 Disclosure and Barring Service.

4 The DBS carries out criminal record checks to help prevent unsuitable people from working with vulnerable adults or children. If the individual is on the 'Barred List', they will not be able to get this type of job.

1.3 The benefits to service users' health and well-being when their rights are maintained (page 22)

1. Empowerment – giving someone the authority or control to do something. This is how a health or social care worker encourages an individual to make decisions and take control of their life and become independent.

   Self-esteem – when a person feels valued and respected. High self-esteem is associated with people who are happy and confident. An individual with low self-esteem can experience feelings of unhappiness and worthlessness.

2. Four from:
   - to empower individuals
   - so that people feel valued
   - to raise self-esteem
   - to instil confidence
   - to instil trust
   - so that individuals feel safe
   - to give equality of access to services
   - to meet individual needs.

3. Three from:
   - High self-esteem – a person feels valued and respected. High self-esteem is associated with people who are happy and confident. An individual with low self-esteem experiences feelings of unhappiness and worthlessness.
   - Empowerment – this gives someone the authority or control to do something. This is how a health or social care worker encourages and enables an individual to make decisions and take control of their life and so become independent.
   - Confidence – individuals will feel that they can rely on care workers and services to get high-quality care that meets their needs.
   - Trust – individuals must be able to feel that care workers are trustworthy, that they will not harm them and that they have the individual's best interests at heart.
   - Equality – individuals will be able to access the care they need. Adaptations will be made if necessary for them to access care.
   - Safety – care workers and care settings support individuals' rights to safety and will follow health and safety laws and ensure staff are trained in safeguarding procedures.

4. Three from:
   - given choices of care
   - choice of where to receive treatment
   - choice of GP
   - whether or not to receive treatment
   - given information about what services are available
   - any other example involving choice or support to meet individual needs.

5. Two from:
   - may not want to continue with the care they should be receiving
   - unable to access the care they need
   - may feel unsafe
   - physical health may deteriorate
   - mental health may deteriorate.

Topic area 2: Person-centred values

2.1 Person-centred values and how they are applied by service providers

Person-centred values (page 27)

1. The diversity of individuals working in and using health and social care services. The people using, and working in, healthcare and social care services are very diverse, that is they are all different.

2. Two from:
   - Support communication needs – for example, provide information in Braille, make hearing loops available, have staff available who can use sign language.
   - Give service users choice – for example, over food/meals.
   - Provide optional activities, resources and food that reflect different cultures, beliefs and faiths.
   - Celebrate a range of religious and non-religious festivals in the care setting, to reflect the different faiths and cultural needs of the service users.

3. Two from:
   - Mobility – ensure all areas of the retirement home and resources are accessible to all by providing, for example, ramps, automatic doors and adjustable-height tables where necessary.
   - Encourage residents' choices – which clothes to wear, which activities to take part in.
   - Provide transport and carers to accompany service users on trips; visit wheelchair-accessible venues.

4. Two from:
   - Keep patient records secure – lock them in a filing cabinet or, if stored electronically, keep them password-protected.
   - Use a private office or empty room for meetings with residents or their family to discuss treatment or care.
   - Do not discuss patients, residents or other service users in public places.
   - Share information with other practitioners only on a 'need-to-know' basis – and only with those directly involved in caring for the individual.

5. Two from:
   - Keep them as fully involved in decision-making as possible.
   - Ask what they would like to happen.

- Ask about their preferences, views.
- Provide an advocate to represent the individual.
- Encourage them to make their own decisions.

6 Four from:
- individuality
- choice
- rights
- independence
- privacy
- dignity
- respect
- partnership
- encouraging decision-making.

Qualities of a service practitioner, the 6Cs (page 29)

1 The six C's are:
- Care
- Compassion
- Competence
- Communication
- Courage
- Commitment

2 Their definitions are:
- Care – a care worker should do all they can to maintain or improve an individual's health and wellbeing
- Compassion – being able to provide care and support with kindness, consideration, respect and empathy.
- Competence – the ability of a care worker to provide high-quality, effective, safe care and support with kindness, consideration, respect and empathy.
- Communication – essential to developing good relationships with service users, their families and also with colleagues. Being able to listen carefully and speak in a way that individuals receiving care and support can understand.
- Courage – being brave and able to speak up about concerns, doing the right thing and also having the courage to try something new, such as new ways of working.
- Commitment is a promise or agreement to do something. It is the responsibility that care workers and practitioners in health and social care services have for those in their care – to perform the tasks and carry out the responsibilities of their particular job role to the required standard and for the benefit of their service users.

3 Any two appropriate examples, such as:
- Care – ensuring dietary needs are met, such as gluten-free, diabetic, vegan.
- Competence – attending regular training to develop skills.
- Commitment – carrying out tasks of the job role to the required standard.
- Communication – listening to residents and taking an interest in what they are saying to develop good relationships.
- Compassion – sitting quietly with an elderly person nearing the end of life.

4 Any two appropriate examples, such as:
- Communication – not using jargon, using understandable language, not specialist terms, when describing treatment to patients.
- Compassion – showing empathy and kindness when a patient is distressed.
- Courage – speaking up if they have any concerns about an individual, perhaps not following their treatment plan, for example.
- Competence – being able to complete accurate and detailed records of treatment provided and the patient's test results.

5 Two appropriate examples, such as:
- Communication – never appearing rushed, taking time, making sure the individual has time to talk if they want to.
- Courage – suggesting how the individual may obtain help to improve their circumstances and deal with their problems.
- Commitment – providing the care and support promised to the individual.
- Competence – ensuring that they have the knowledge and understanding to provide appropriate care for homeless individuals.

2.2 Benefits of applying the person-centred values (page 31)

1 Any from:
- Empowerment is giving someone the ability or control to enable them to do something.
- This is how a health or social care worker encourages an individual to make decisions and take control of their life and become independent.
- The process that enables individuals to take control of their lives and make their own decisions.
- Giving someone confidence in their own abilities.

2 Two from:
- The service user's individual needs are met, for example: adaptations to the environment, correct care provided.
- For example, helping a patient to recover or be as comfortable and independent as possible.
- Ensures the service user is involved in decision-making by discussing their care needs.

3 Four from:
- Provides clear guidelines of the standards of care that should be provided.
- Improves job satisfaction.
- Maintains and improves quality of care provided.
- Supports rights to choice and consultation.
- Supports practitioners to develop their skills.
- Enables the sharing of good practice.

2.3 Effects on service users' health and wellbeing if person-centred values are not applied (page 35)

1 The four definitions are:
   - Physical effects relate to an individual's body.
   - Intellectual means an individual's thought processes, such as thinking skills, understanding, learning, reasoning, comprehension and knowledge.
   - Emotional effects relate to an individual's feelings.
   - Social effects on people if the values of care are not applied relate to an individual's relationship with others.

2 Two each from:
   - Physical:
     - dehydration
     - thirst
     - illness gets worse
     - delays recovery.
   - Emotional:
     - upset
     - feeling unimportant/devalued
     - distressed
     - anxious.

3 Possible descriptions:
   - anger, annoyance that her request is not taken seriously
   - frustration because she does not know why she cannot have a home birth
   - upset she cannot have the home birth
   - devalued because she has not been offered an explanation.

4 Example explanations could include:
   - Physically Jayson might be injured by the bully – bruises, broken bones, etc.
   - Socially he may not want to join in with others; he may want to just stay at home; he might develop behaviour problems and aggression towards others.
   - Emotionally he may become withdrawn and not want to attend the day centre; he might feel unsafe and become very unhappy and scared.
   - Intellectually he might lack concentration; this could slow his progress and lead to him underachieving; time off from the day centre would also limit his progress and development of skills.

Topic area 3: Effective communication skills in health and social care settings

3.1 The importance of verbal communication skills in health and social care settings (page 37)

1 Any four from:
   - clarity
   - empathy
   - patience
   - using appropriate vocabulary
   - tone
   - volume
   - pace
   - willingness to contribute to team working.

2 Explanations could include:
   - Clarity – information that is clearly stated and is understandable.
   - Empathy – the ability to imagine yourself in another person's situation and understand how they might be thinking or feeling. This can help a care worker to gain a better understanding of another person and lets the service user know that their feelings have been acknowledged.
   - Patience – not making a service user feel pressured, giving them the time to say what they need and want. Repeating if necessary so they can take in the information.
   - Using appropriate vocabulary – straightforward medical or other information is given and any specialist terms are avoided, or if not they are explained in simplified everyday terms. Jargon that only health or social care professionals would understand is not used as far as possible.
   - Tone – a positive and even tone of voice that is not too loud or too quiet, is friendly, calm and reassuring.
   - Volume – speaking too loudly can be assertive or domineering. It can also breach confidentiality if people can overhear. Care workers should choose a tone of voice suitable to where the conversation is taking place and based on the situation, for example speaking to a patient about test results or delivering a training session to a group of staff will require a different volume to be used.

- Pace – important information will be missed if a care worker speaks too quickly. For example, at a shift handover on a hospital ward, it is vital that the health and progress of all patients is clearly understood by the incoming staff, so this should not be rushed. It is important to use an appropriate pace that gives others enough time to take in information or instructions.
- Willingness to contribute to team working – teams of staff do not always work together face to face; they can communicate with each other through conference calls, patient records, emails and telephone calls – this enables the necessary information to be shared.

3 Two from:
- finding out about a person's symptoms
- explaining test results
- giving bad news to a patient or their family
- consoling someone who is upset
- responding to questions
- responding to complaints
- calming someone down
- discussing individuals' treatment and progress with the care team.

4 Three from:
- the service user is sensory impaired – deaf/blind
- the service user speaks a different language from the care worker
- someone with learning difficulties
- someone with dementia
- consoling someone who is upset
- calming someone down
- giving bad news
- responding to a complaint
- explaining test results
- or any other appropriate situations.

3.2 The importance of non-verbal communication skills in health and social care settings (page 39)

1 The five types of non-verbal communication:
- Eye contact – showing interest, acknowledging what has been said.
- Gestures – thumbs up or down, wave hello/goodbye, pointing something out.
- Facial expression – interested, reassurance, agreement.
- Body language – positive/open, no crossed arms.
- Sense of humour – being able to see the funny side of things.

2 Positioning:
- Some positions can create physical and emotional barriers that inhibit effective communication.
- If a service user cannot see the care worker properly because of where they are standing, it does not support good communication.
- Emotionally, having someone leaning over and looking down on them can make a service user feel insignificant and powerless because they feel dominated.

Height:
- It is preferable if a person is at the same level as the practitioner who is talking with them. If the practitioner, for example a social worker, is standing and the service user is sitting, they may feel dominated by the social worker, as though they are being talked down to. This does not help effective communication to take place.

3 Being able to see the funny side of things can create a more relaxed atmosphere, puts people at their ease and makes them feel more relaxed.

3.3 The importance of active listening skills in health and social care settings (page 41)

1 For example:
- Active listening is an effective method of listening to build rapport, trust and understanding between those involved.
- The use of active listening by a care practitioner involves demonstrating an interest in and responsiveness to what a person is saying by fully concentrating on what is being said rather than just passively 'hearing'.

2
- Open, relaxed posture.
- Eye contact, looking interested.
- Nodding agreement.
- Showing empathy, reflecting feelings.
- Clarifying.
- Summarising to show understanding of key points.

3
- Helps them to gather information needed to inform the type of care required.
- Helps them to get to know the individual.
- They will be aware of the service user's needs, preferences and choices.
- Allows carers to identify and plan to meet the individual's needs.

4
- They will feel secure that the service provider has listened and is aware of the type of care they need.
- They will feel respected as individuals.
- They will feel empowered as they will have had the opportunity to express their needs, worries and preferences.
- It establishes co-operation, trust and involvement in a care partnership.

3.4 The importance of special methods of communication in health and social care settings

Advocate (page 43)

1 One appropriate situation, such as:
   - If the teenager is being removed from their family due to a child protection issue, an advocate could ensure that the teenager's preference as to who they wish to stay with is heard.
   - At a meeting to discuss a bullying issue, an advocate could provide support.

2 Three appropriate examples, such as:
   - go with an individual to meetings or attend for them
   - help an individual to find and access information
   - write letters on the individual's behalf
   - represent an individual's views at a case conference.

3 For example:

Advocacy	Supports right to:
Individuals have their needs, views and preferences taken into account.	Consultation
Individuals have their voice heard.	Choice/consultation
Defends and promotes the rights of individuals with learning, physical and mental disabilities.	Equal and fair treatment. Protection from abuse and harm

4 An advocate will not:
   - judge the individual
   - give their personal opinion
   - make decisions for the individual.

Special methods of communicating (page 44)

1 Verbal:
   - telephone call
   - meeting
   - conversation
   - discussion
   - questions/interview
   - online meeting.

   Non-verbal:
   - gestures
   - facial expressions
   - eye contact
   - sign language (BSL)
   - Braille
   - care plan.

2 Descriptions could include:
   - repetition
   - being patient
   - slow pace
   - simple vocabulary, short sentences
   - use of picture cards
   - not being patronising
   - use of positive body language
   - concentrate on what they are saying.

3 Explanations could include:
   - aids understanding of procedures/treatment/what's happening, etc
   - the individual feels valued
   - instils confidence
   - develops trust
   - shows respect
   - shows you are listening
   - the individual feels they are being taken seriously
   - enables informed decisions/choices to be made
   - provides equality of access
   - empowers individuals
   - raises self-esteem
   - helps to meet the individual's needs.

4 Possible ways could include:
   - use of facial expression
   - use of body language/gestures
   - being patient and calm/repeating as necessary
   - using pictures
   - providing leaflets/printed information in Polish
   - providing an interpreter/translator
   - finding another member of staff or relative/friend who can speak Polish
   - use 'Language Line'.

3.5 The importance of effective communication in health and social care settings (page 47)

1 Three from:
   - Emphasise important words.
   - Slow the pace of conversation if necessary.
   - Increase the tone of voice but not do not shout.
   - Use repetition where appropriate.
   - Use gestures or flash cards/pictures if appropriate.
   - Make use of aids to communication such as a hearing loop system.
   - Use specialist communication methods such as Braille or signing.
   - Use technological aids, such as Dynavox or a Lightwriter.

2

Methods of effective communication	How they support rights and person-centred values
• Avoid jargon. • Explain any specialist terminology. • Use age-appropriate vocabulary. • Use simplified language, for example with young children, individuals with learning disabilities or patients with dementia. • Use interpreters or translators.	Using vocabulary that can be understood by all
• Use positive body language, such as nodding agreement and making eye contact. • Avoid sarcasm and do not talk down to the person. • Be polite. • Make the service user feel they are being taken seriously. • Be patient, especially when listening to repetition. • Do not ignore the person's views or beliefs just because they are different from yours.	Use communication that is appropriate to the individual
• Use active listening by demonstrating interest in response to what a person is saying, using body language to show a positive reaction. • Ask the person rather than assuming you know what they want, need or prefer. • Concentrate on what the person is saying – this can encourage them to communicate their needs.	Listen to individual's needs/active listening
• Emphasise important words. • Slow the pace of conversation if necessary. • Increase tone of voice but not do not shout. • Use repetition where appropriate. • Using gestures or flash cards/pictures if appropriate. • Make use of aids to communication such as a hearing loop system. • Use specialist communication methods such as Braille or signing. • Use technological aids, such as Dynavox or a Lightwriter.	Adapt communication to meet individual's needs/situation

3 Three from:
   • Misunderstanding if information is not clearly explained.
   • Errors or danger to health due to inaccurate record keeping.
   • Distress and upset if the service user feels patronised.
   • If speech is too fast or unfamiliar vocabulary is used, the listener will not be able to take it all in.

Accept other examples of appropriate impacts.

4 Individuals:
   • with a learning disability
   • with a physical disability
   • who have had a stroke
   • who are visually or hearing impaired
   • whose first language is different from the care worker's
   • who are shy and introverted and who may not enjoy communicating information with new staff.

Topic area 4: Protecting service users and service providers in health and social care settings

4.1 Safeguarding

Service users who need safeguarding (page 51)

1 Six from:
   • children
   • people with physical and/or learning disabilities
   • people with mental health conditions
   • older adults dependent on carers in residential settings
   • people with a sensory impairment – sight or hearing loss
   • children in residential care dependent on carers
   • older adults in residential care
   • vulnerable groups such as homeless people.

2 For many reasons these individuals may not want to, or be able to, report poor care or abuse.
   • They are dependent on carers and may not want to upset them as their treatment might get worse.
   • They may not know or understand their rights.
   • They may not even realise they are being abused.
   • They may not see or hear who is abusing them.
   • They may lack mental capacity due to dementia and may not understand what is happening.
   • Someone who is homeless may not have any support, from family for example.
   These reasons may apply to more than one group.

3 Three from:
   • protecting children from maltreatment – e.g. physical, emotional, psychological abuse

- preventing impairment of children's health and development – physical health and well-being, education
- ensuring children grow up in a stable home with the provision of safe and effective care – removal from neglect, unstable and chaotic family life
- taking action to enable all children to have the best outcomes – provision of support for the family, fostering or adoption.

4 Three from:

Maladministration of medication	• Incorrect, late or inappropriate medication, e.g. sedatives, pain relief, can result in unrelieved pain and suffering, slow recovery or further illness if medication is inappropriate.
Inadequate care and neglect	• Individuals who are frail or who have restricted mobility are at risk of developing sores on the points of their body which receive the most pressure. People need to be moved often to avoid sores developing. • Lack of regular meals and drinks can result in malnutrition and dehydration. • Rough treatment, or being rushed, shouted at, or ignored.
Falls	• Residents not being assessed on their risk of falls; walking aids not provided.
Poor nutritional care	• Inappropriate food provided for chewing and swallowing problems, religious or dietary needs, resulting in malnutrition.
Lack of social inclusion	• No stimulation, activity, opportunities for social interaction.

Institutional abuse	• Occurs when the routines and systems of an organisation result in poor or inadequate standards of care and poor practice.
	• This affects the whole setting:
	  • It denies, restricts or ignores the dignity, privacy, choice and independence of individuals.
	  • For example, people being forced to eat or go to bed at a particular time in a residential home.
	  • Verbal abuse if the individual does not co-operate with procedures.

Physical abuse	• Between residents or staff and residents.
Financial abuse	• For example, theft of personal money or possessions, staff inappropriately accepting gifts.

5 Three from:
- Equipment is old and/or damaged, e.g. hoists, toys, and so could cause injury.
- Activities and visits are not risk assessed so potential risks and ways of avoiding them are not identified.
- Staff are not trained in how to use equipment and so may injure themselves or those in their care, e.g. when transferring someone out of a bath using a hoist.
- Staff are not trained in how to carry out manual handling safely and so may injure someone they are caring for, or themselves, while helping them out of bed into a chair, for example.
- Staff are not trained in providing intimate care, e.g. bathing, changing continence pads, and so may be accused of abuse due to not following correct procedures.
- There is a shortage of staff so they are rushed and unable to take the time required with their service users, who are then neglected, or staff may get impatient and use verbal abuse if, for example, someone with dementia is taking 'too long' to get dressed.
- There is a lack of diversity and equality training so incidents involving prejudice and discrimination are more likely to occur.
- Staff are not given safeguarding training and so are unaware of their role in dealing with suspected abuse or harm.
- Staff are not DBS checked and so it is not known if they have a criminal record and have been barred from working with vulnerable adults and children and so they may be a risk to individuals in their care.

Safeguarding procedures in care settings (page 54)

1 Three reasons:
- All care settings are required by law to have safeguarding policies and procedures in place.
- The policy must state the ways of working and procedures to follow regarding any safeguarding issues.
- All staff must be trained so they are familiar with the policy and so they are aware of what to do if anyone makes a disclosure of abuse.

2 Designated Safeguarding Lead.

3 The role of the DSL includes:
- creating the care setting's safeguarding policy
- reviewing the setting's plan for safeguarding
- ensuring all staff know how to raise safeguarding concerns
- referring concerns over an individual's welfare to social services, police, the CQC or other appropriate organisation
- providing training so all staff understand the signs and symptoms of abuse and neglect
- gathering any evidence or information about incidents of abuse or neglect.

4
- Recognise
- Respond
- Report
- Record
- Refer

Exam-style question answers at www.hoddereducation.co.uk/myrevisionnotesdownloads

5 Three from:
- Listen to the disclosure – do not ask questions.
- Write it down as soon as possible, in the person's own words.
- Reassure the individual they've done the right thing.
- Inform them you will write down what they have said and will pass it on so that the abuse/harm can be dealt with, on a 'need-to-know' basis.

Disclosure and Barring Service (page 55)

1 DBS checks ensure that individuals are safe to work or volunteer with vulnerable adults and children. The checks prevent anyone who is not suitable from working with individuals who have support needs such as learning disabilities or dementia, or who need health or personal care, for example.

2
- Disclosure and Barring Service checks are a requirement for anyone over 16 for roles that involve working or volunteering with children or vulnerable adults.
- Anyone applying to foster or adopt a child.

3 Standard, Enhanced and Enhanced with list checks.

4
- Standard – checks for criminal convictions, cautions, reprimands and final warnings.
- Enhanced – an additional check of any information held by police that is relevant to the role being applied for.
- Enhanced with list checks – this additionally checks the 'barred list'.

5
- This is a list of individuals who are on record as being unsuitable for working with children or vulnerable adults.
- Therefore, they are 'barred', that is, not allowed to do this kind of work.

4.2 Infection prevention

General cleanliness (page 57)

1 Three from:
- spillages cleared straight away, e.g. vomit, urine, blood, and the area cleaned and disinfected
- equipment sterilised
- hazardous waste disposed of following correct procedures – e.g. used sharps (needles) in a hard yellow sharps box
- specialist disposal methods such as yellow bags for used dressings, disposable gloves and other clinical waste
- bathrooms and toilets cleaned and disinfected frequently
- all used antiseptic wipes and tissues disposed of immediately after use into a covered bin.

2 Descriptions of good hygiene practices include:
- Wearing a cleaners uniform protects from cross-contamination.
- Range of cleaning materials and equipment shows evidence of a thorough approach to cleaning.
- Disposable gloves protect from the spread of infection and protect hands from the effects of detergents on the skin.

3 Descriptions could include:
- use of anti-bacterial sprays or wipes on work surfaces, door handles, computer keyboards
- equipment for activities cleaned regularly
- toilets cleaned and disinfected frequently
- floors mopped and carpets vacuumed every day
- bins emptied and cleaned frequently.

4 Example reasons:
- Bacteria accumulate on people's hands throughout the day as they touch surfaces, equipment, etc., so infection can easily spread through using a computer that is used by multiple people.
- If residents, nurses or admin staff do not wash hands frequently enough, bacteria will transfer onto everything the person touches.
- Many different people will be using the computer through the day which increases the risk of spreading infection.
- Computer keyboards have lots of places where bacteria can easily build up.

Personal hygiene measures (page 59)

1 Practices to keep yourself clean in order to prevent illness and the spread of disease.

2
- Jewellery can trap bacteria.
- Not wearing it removes places for bacteria to be trapped.
- Jewellery can scratch, for example when lifting and handling patients.
- Jewellery can get caught on things, and possibly cause injury.
- Nail polish can chip or flake off into food or into a patient's wound, for example.
- Not wearing nail polish prevents contamination.

3 Explanations could include:
- they are not exposed to bacteria from other service users the practitioner has been caring for
- reduces levels of cross-contamination
- less risk of suffering from food poisoning
- infections will not spread as easily.

4 Explanations could include:
- reduces the spread of infection
- will not pass on bacteria to their service users
- prevents illness
- clean hair and teeth carry fewer bacteria.

5 Any four from:
- hair tied back or covered
- regular showering
- regular hair washing
- regular brushing of teeth
- correct hand washing routines
- open wounds covered
- no jewellery
- no nail polish.

Hand washing routines (page 61)

1 Any four from:
   - before putting on and after removing disposable gloves
   - before and after treating wounds or caring for a sick or injured person
   - before and after providing personal care for an individual such as feeding them or helping them get dressed
   - before and after changing a nappy or continence pad
   - before and after preparing or handling any food
   - after handling clinical waste
   - after clearing up rubbish and putting it in the bin
   - after clearing up toys or equipment
   - after using a tissue to blow their nose
   - after touching their face or hair
   - after using the toilet.
2 Aspects to include:
   - wet hands, soap
   - palms and back of hands
   - fingers
   - tips of fingers
   - wrists
   - rinsing and drying.
3 Explanations should include:
   - the most common way of spreading bacteria is by the hands
   - germs accumulate on the hands
   - an individual touches surfaces, objects and people throughout the day
   - frequently washing hands limits the transfer of bacteria and viruses
   - hand washing reduces the chance of spreading infection.

Personal protective equipment (PPE) (page 63)

1 Three from:
   - disposable aprons
   - disposable gloves
   - rubber gloves
   - face masks
   - hairnet or hygiene hat
   - overalls
   - overshoes.
2 Three from:
   - changing incontinence pads
   - changing soiled bed linen
   - dressing wounds
   - clearing up spillages, e.g. vomit, blood
   - food preparation and serving.
3 Possible reasons:
   - Particularly important when preparing or serving food.
   - If hair is not tied back or covered it is more likely to fall into food.
   - If hair is not covered staff are more likely to touch their hair, which can spread bacteria to food.
4
   - It is an effective barrier for retaining droplets that can be released when talking, sneezing or coughing.
   - Along with surgical garments and overshoes face masks reduce the likelihood of contamination during procedures such as surgery or dental work.
5 Protective clothing:
   - hygiene hats
   - overalls
   - aprons.
   Good practice because:
   - hair is covered
   - clean overalls carry fewer bacteria than own clothes
   - aprons provide a second hygienic layer.

4.3 Safety procedures and measures (page 66)

1 A procedure is a process, not a specific action. Safety procedures are guidelines about how to deal with emergency situations such as fire. A procedure informs care workers and service users about what they have to do and how it how it should be done to ensure everyone's safety.

A safety measure is a specific action such as putting up a fire safety notice or using a 'wet floor' sign after mopping the floor in order to provide people with safety information or a warning.

2 Four from:
   - Staff DBS checked to ensure they are suitable and safe to work with children.
   - Staff trained to deal with safeguarding procedures so they know what to do if they suspect abuse, for example.
   - Have trained first aiders to provide emergency treatment for the children.
   - All activities, trips, equipment are risk assessed so that dangers and hazards are minimised and everyone is kept safe.
   - Appropriate levels of supervision depending on the age of the children and the activity taking place.
   - Fire drills practised regularly so that staff are aware of what to do to evacuate the children quickly and efficiently and so the children know where to go in the event of a fire.
3
   - Criminal record checks.
   - Carried out by the Disclosure and Barring Service (DBS).
   - Help prevent unsuitable people working with vulnerable adults or children.
4 Three from:
   - ensures staff know their responsibilities in an emergency
   - enables staff to take quick and efficient action
   - service users will know what to do in an emergency
   - everyone will learn where the assembly points are

Exam-style question answers at www.hoddereducation.co.uk/myrevisionnotesdownloads

- everyone will recognise what the fire alarm sounds like
- ensures everyone evacuates the building and is kept safe.

5 Two from:
- alerts staff to potential dangers
- enables staff to do their job safely
- staff know their specific roles in emergencies
- staff will know how to carry out risk assessments of activities, equipment, etc.
- reduces risks and ensures a safer environment.

Procedures for reducing risks and promoting good practice (page 68)

1 Two from:
- manual handling
- fire evacuation
- risk assessment
- accident reporting
- safeguarding.

2
- good practice
- creates a safe and secure environment
- everyone is working within the law
- everyone kept safe
- minimises risks and dangers.

3 Three from:
- develop the skills and knowledge to avoid injuries to themselves and service users
- gain awareness of security measures used to keep individuals safe
- understand how to apply the values of care
- develop knowledge of effective communication
- carry out first aid
- understand safeguarding procedures
- have knowledge of health and safety policies and procedures
- carry out risk assessments
- carry out moving and handling techniques safely.

4 Example policies include:
- accident reporting
- bullying
- confidentiality
- equal opportunities
- fire evacuation
- health and safety
- manual handling
- risk assessment
- safeguarding.

Risk assessments (page 69)

1 A hazard is anything that could cause harm. Risk is the likelihood that someone or something could be harmed.
2 An action that can be taken to reduce the risks posed by a hazard or to remove the hazard altogether.
3 The process of evaluating the likelihood of a hazard actually causing harm.

- Step 1: Look for hazards associated with the activity.
- Step 2: Identify who might be harmed and how.
- Step 3: Consider the level of risk – decide on the precautions or control measures needed to reduce the risk.
- Step 4: Make a written record of the findings.
- Step 5: Review the risk assessment regularly and improve precautions or control measures if necessary.

4 Three from:
- items lying around on the floor
- frayed carpet
- a rug
- wet floor
- trailing cables
- blocked fire exit
- cleaning materials not stored securely
- electrical equipment not PAT tested.

Moving and handling techniques (page 72)

1 Four from:
- transferring a patient from a hospital bed to a chair
- assisting an elderly person with their mobility, for example helping them to get out of a chair or into a bath or shower
- arranging tables and chairs in a nursery
- carrying boxes of toys/equipment
- pushing trolleys, drip stands, wheelchairs, etc.
- moving a commode into an elderly person's bedroom
- a home care assistant carrying shopping bags.

2 Example reasons why:
- so that they can give you permission to carry out the move
- so that the person knows what you are going to do
- makes them feel valued
- helps them be more relaxed and less anxious about being moved
- makes the move smoother and easier to carry out if the individual knows what to expect
- builds a trusting relationship between practitioner and service user.

3 Procedure:
- Preferably use appropriate equipment – trolley, box on wheels – rather than lift.
- Only lift as much as can be easily carried – do not lift as much as you can, this can cause injury.
- Check that there are no dangers in the environment such as an uneven or slippery floor and that there is enough space to carry out the move.
- Bend the knees, avoid twisting the back or moving sideways.
- Keep feet wide apart for stability.
- Hold the item being lifted close to the body.
- Move smoothly, not jerkily – this reduces the risk of injury.

4 Three from:
- always check whether the move or lift is really necessary – do not carry out a move unless it is unavoidable.
- identify any risks involved in carrying out the move and take steps to avoid or minimise risks identified.
- use a lifting aid if appropriate rather than carry out the lift yourself.
- if the move has been assessed to require two people, do not attempt the move on your own.
- only carry out manual handing if you have been trained to do so.

5 Three from:
- manual handling training provides staff with guidance on good practice so they will know how to lift and move individuals safely – this gives them more confidence.
- risks to service users and staff will be assessed and minimised.
- staff will know if a second person is need for the manual handling task.
- staff will do their job correctly – this ensures a safer environment.
- service users will have more confidence in staff who have been trained in manual handling – this will help them relax when being moved because they trust the staff.
- prevents injuries to both service users and care workers.
- being trained protects staff from accusations of abuse as correct techniques will be used so service users will feel comfortable and they will be treated with dignity and respect.

Emergency procedures (page 74)

1 Four from:
- how to raise the alarm
- who calls 999
- staff roles in the evacuation
- the special arrangements for certain individuals – hearing impaired, people with mobility difficulties, dementia patients
- checks that need to be carried out – empty rooms, windows closed, switch off lights
- where to assemble
- carry out head count, check register.

2 Discussion points:

For service providers:
- ensures that they can keep everyone as safe as possible and away from danger
- ensures the care setting complies with health and safety legislation
- provides guidance for staff so that they know exactly what to do in an emergency
- enables staff to take quick and efficient action to remove service users and themselves from danger.

For service users:
- provides guidance so that they know what to do in an emergency
- individuals using services will be reassured by knowing these procedures exist to help them in an emergency
- awareness that staff are trained to deal with emergency situations reduces anxiety for service users
- instils trust that service provider is professional and cares for service users.

3 Four from:
- fire safety notices throughout the care setting
- signs indicating fire exits
- signs indicating assembly points
- a fire extinguisher by each exit
- a fire blanket in kitchen areas.

4
- In case of health emergencies care settings must have enough trained first aiders available for the number of staff and service users.
- The specific health needs of the service users would also be taken into account.

Equipment considerations (page 76)

1
- The toys should be checked for small or loose components that could be choking hazards.
- Ensure that the toys are age appropriate – look for the age advice symbol.
- Check that the toys have appropriate safety labels: BSI or Lion Mark.

2
- Faults are spotted early as staff know it is their responsibility to report problems.
- Repairs are carried out as soon as they are needed.
- Equipment is not out of use for long as it will be known there is a problem.
- Items will be disposed of and replaced or repaired as appropriate.
- Equipment is well maintained and kept in good condition so less chance of it causing injuries or breaking down when in use.
- Equipment is serviced regularly and so kept in good working order.

3 Portable Appliance Testing is the term used to describe the checking of electrical appliances and equipment to ensure they are safe to use.

4
- Correct equipment is provided for the task.
- Staff are trained and so know how to use the equipment correctly – this prevents injuries to themselves or to the service users.
- Specialist equipment is available when needed, for example hoists, fire evacuation chairs, etc., so that service users are handled safely.
- Electrical equipment is safe so the risk of injury is reduced.
- Ensures the care setting is complying with health and safety legislation.

Exam-style question answers at www.hoddereducation.co.uk/myrevisionnotesdownloads

4.4 How security measures protect service users and staff (page 79)

1. Explanation points:
   - Lanyards quickly identify staff.
   - Easy to spot unauthorised people without a lanyard/badge who can then be challenged.
   - Easy to identify visitors.
   - Visitors will know who is a member of staff.
   - Improves safety – no strangers or intruders.
2. Four from:
   - having a member of staff on duty at the reception desk
   - locks on external doors
   - monitoring of keys
   - security pads with pin codes
   - electronic swipe card entry system
   - CCTV monitoring exits and entrances
   - alarms on external doors that are not in regular use
   - window locks and window restraints.
3. Four from:
   - staff on duty at the reception desk
   - signing in and out book for visitors
   - escorting visitors
   - issuing visitor badges
   - staff wearing ID lanyards
   - staff uniform
   - window locks and window restraints
   - CCTV monitoring exits and entrances
   - alarms on external doors that are not in regular use.
4.
   - A limited number of people will have keys so access is controlled.
   - Having a list of 'key holders' ensures the whereabouts of all sets of keys is known at all times.
   - Prevents intruders from entering the building.

Glossary

Advocate Someone who speaks on behalf of an individual who is unable to speak up for themselves. Page 16

Anaphylactic shock An extreme allergic reaction. Common causes can be nuts, celery, seafood, and wasp or bee stings. Page 74

Bacteria Tiny, microscopic organisms. Some bacteria can cause infection and disease. Page 58

Body language A type of non-verbal communication through body posture, facial expressions, gestures and eye contact. Page 36

Braille A method of communication used by visually impaired or blind people that consists of raised dots which are read by touch. Page 36

Cannulas Thin tubes that surround a flexible needle that is inserted into a vein to administer medication from a drip. Page 56

Care setting Anywhere where care is provided. Different care settings provide different types of care. Page 10

Confidentiality Limits access to or places restrictions on sharing certain types of sensitive information so that it is kept private and can only be accessed by those who need to be aware of it. Page 14

Consultation The process of discussing something with someone in order to get their advice or opinion, so that a decision can be made that is acceptable to all involved. Page 16

Contamination When something is tainted with other substances that may be unclean – for example, disease-causing bacteria. Page 59

Control measures Actions that can be taken to reduce the risks posed by a hazard or to remove the hazard altogether. Page 68

CQC Care Quality Commission – a government organisation that registers, licenses and inspects health and social care services. Page 53

Cross-contamination When bacteria spread onto food from another source, such as hands, work surfaces, kitchen equipment and utensils, or between cooked and raw food. Page 59

DBS checks Criminal record checks carried out by the Disclosure and Barring Service to help prevent unsuitable people working in health and social care services. Page 19

Disclosure When an individual tells you directly, or indirectly through their behaviour, that they have been, or are being, abused. Page 53

Discrimination The unjust and unfair treatment of individuals based on their differences, such as race, religious beliefs, disability or gender. Page 19

Disempowerment Feeling that you have a lack of control over your life and lack independence. Page 33

Diversity The recognition that everyone is different and has different needs, so appreciating and respecting individual differences such as a person's faith, diet, ethnicity and customs. Page 19

Empathy Having the ability to identify with another person's situation and understand how they may be feeling or thinking. Page 28

Empowerment The process that enables individuals to take control of their lives and make their own decisions; giving someone confidence in their own abilities. Page 31

Epipen An emergency treatment for someone with a severe anaphylactic reaction. It is an automatic injector device which contains a dose of the hormone adrenaline, which is injected into the thigh. Page 74

Equality Enabling individuals to have the same rights, access and opportunities as everyone else regardless of gender, race, ability, age, sexual orientation or religious belief. Page 19

Equality Act A law which aims to ensure service users are treated fairly. Page 12

Gluten free A diet that does not include the grains wheat, barley and rye, which can trigger a dietary intolerance in some individuals. Page 13

Halal A diet in which no pork is eaten and all meat has to be prepared according to Muslim law. Page 13

Hazard Anything that could cause harm, e.g. a faulty piece of equipment or a particular activity. Page 67

Hygiene Practices that keep you and your surroundings clean in order to prevent illness and the spread of disease. Page 58

Inclusion Involving people in their care to ensure they are treated fairly and are not excluded, for example making care services accessible by providing disability access such as wheelchair ramps or information in Braille or a range of different languages. Page 25

Infection When bacteria (germs) invade the body and cause a disease or illness. Page 58

Jargon Specialist or technical language or terms and abbreviations that are difficult for non-specialists to understand. Page 37

Exam-style question answers at **www.hoddereducation.co.uk/myrevisionnotesdownloads**

Kosher In Judaism, this is used to describe something that is 'correct' – that is, food is sold, cooked or eaten satisfying the requirements of Jewish law. Meat and dairy cannot be eaten at the same time. Page 13

Laws Passed by Parliament and state the rights and entitlements of service users. If someone breaks the law, they can be prosecuted by being taken to court. Page 12

Learned helplessness When someone gives up trying as a result of consistent lack of achievement or reward – they come to believe that it is not trying because they will fail anyway. Page 34

Manual Handling Using the correct procedures when physically moving any load by lifting, putting down, pushing or pulling – for example, transferring a patient from a chair to a bed. Page 19

Marginalised Excluded from participating; feeling unimportant and not wanted by the majority of people. Page 34

Need-to-know basis Information is shared only with those directly involved with the care and support of an individual. Page 14

PAT tested Stands for 'Portable Appliance Testing'; used to describe the checking of electrical appliances and equipment to ensure they are safe to use. Page 32

Posture The position in which someone holds their body when standing or sitting. Page 40

Prejudice A dislike of, or negative attitude towards, an individual, often based on ill-informed personal opinion. Examples include racial prejudice and homophobia. Page 19

Risk The likelihood that someone or something could be harmed. Page 67

Risk assessment The process of evaluating the likelihood of a hazard actually causing harm. Page 67

Safeguarding Measures taken to reduce the risks of danger, harm and abuse. Page 19

Security measures All the actions taken within a care setting to protect individuals – for example, controlling access and identifying staff and visitors. Page 19

Sensory impairment When one of the senses (sight, hearing, touch, smell, taste and special awareness) does not function normally. For example, if you wear glasses then you have sight impairment; if you wear a hearing aid then you have a hearing impairment. Page 49

Self-esteem How much a person values themselves and the life they live. Page 13

Sharps Examples include used needles and cannulas. Page 56

Sharps injury When the skin is punctured by a needle or blade, such as a scalpel, or other medical instrument. Page 66

Sonographer A health professional who is specially trained to carry out ultrasound scans. Page 45

Special educational needs Children with learning or physical disabilities, for example hearing or visual impairments, or conditions such as ADHD or autism. Page 18

Vegetarian A diet in which no meat or fish is eaten. Page 13

Vulnerable Someone who is less able to protect themselves from harm due to, for example, mental health problems or a physical or learning disability. Page 50

Index

abuse
  disclosure of 53
  financial 50
  institutional 50
  physical 50
  protection from 19–20
accessibility 17–18, 26
accident prevention 66–72
active listening 40–1, 46
advocate 16, 42–3
anaphylactic shock 74
bacteria 57–8
body language 36, 38
Braille 27, 36, 43
British Sign Language (BSL) 43
bullying 32, 50
cannulas 56
Care Certificate 28
Care Quality Commission (CQC) 19, 53
care settings *see* settings
charities 11, 43
choice 13, 16, 25
cleanliness 56–7
command words 8
commitment 28
communication 27, 28, 36–47
  advocacy 16, 42–3
  aids 43–4
  barriers to 46
  listening skills 40–1, 46
  non-verbal 36, 38–9
  verbal 36–7
compassion 28
competence 28
confidence 22, 34
confidentiality 14–15
consultation 16–17
contamination 59
context-based questions 7
courage 28
cross-contamination 59
decision-making 26, 31

Index

dehydration 32
depression 32
Designated Safeguarding Lead (DSL) 19, 53
diet 13, 27, 50
dignity 26
disabilities 17–18
Disclosure and Barring Service (DBS) 19–20, 51, 55
discrimination 19, 26–7
disempowerment 33–4
diversity 19, 51
domiciliary care 10
duty of care 50
emergency procedures 64, 72–4
emotional health 10, 21, 33–4
empathy 28, 37
empowerment 21, 31
Epipen 74
Equality Act 2010 12, 18
equal treatment 17–18, 22, 51
equipment 74–5
evacuation procedures 64, 73
exam countdown 5
eye contact 38, 40
fair treatment 17–18
falls 50
financial abuse 50
fire procedures 72–3
first aid 73–4
five Rs 54
food preparation 59
General Data Protection Regulation (GDPR) 2018 14
gluten free diet 13
good practice 30
Halal diet 13
hand washing 60–1
hazards 20, 32, 56, 67–9
health and safety 19, 22, 32, 51
   accident prevention 66–72
   equipment 75
   personal hygiene 58–61
   risk assessment 67–9
   safety measures 65
   safety procedures 64
Health and Safety at Work etc Act 1974 19, 64, 68
healthcare settings 10, 13, 56
hearing loop 43
hygiene 58
inclusion 25
independence 26
individuality 25
individual needs 21
individual rights see rights of service users
infection, definition 58

infection prevention
   cleanliness 56–7
   food preparation 59
   hand washing 60–1
   personal hygiene 58–61
   personal protective equipment (PPE) 61–3
injuries 32, 66
institutional abuse 50
interpreter 43
jargon 37
Kosher food 13
language 27, 37
learned helplessness 34
legislation
   Equality Act 2010 12, 18
   General Data Protection Regulation (GDPR) 2018 14
   Health and Safety at Work etc Act 1974 19, 64, 68
   laws, definition 12
   Manual Handling Operations Regulations (1992) 69
listening skills 40–1, 46
Makaton 43
maladministration of medication 50
malnutrition 32, 50
manual handling 19, 51, 66, 69–72
Manual Handling Operations Regulations (1992) 69
marginalisation 34
medication, maladministration of 50
mental health 10–11, 15, 21, 32–4, 42–3
moving and handling see manual handling
need-to-know basis 14–15
neglect 50
non-verbal communication 36, 38–9
partnership 26
patience 37
personal hygiene 58–61
personal protective equipment (PPE) 61–3
personal space 38
person-centred practice 24
person-centred values 24–7, 29–34
physical abuse 50
picture exchange communication system (PECS) 43
PIES effects 32–5, 52
policies and procedures 19, 67
   safeguarding 53
   safety procedures 64
Portable Appliance Testing (PAT) 32
practitioner qualities 28
prejudice 19
privacy 26

quality of care 29–30
quality of life 30–1
religion 13, 26–7
residential settings 11, 13
respect 26
rights of service users 12–22, 25
risk 67
risk assessment 67–9
safeguarding 19–20, 32, 49–50
   common issues 50
   disclosure of abuse 53
   five Rs 54
   policies and procedures 53
   training 19–20, 51, 53–4
safety measures 65
safety procedures 64
security measures 19, 77–8
self-confidence 34
self-esteem 13, 21
self-harm 32
sensory impairment 49
service users
   decision-making 26, 31
   needs of 21
   physical health 32
   quality of life 30–1
   rights of 12–22, 25
   vulnerable 50
settings
   healthcare 10, 13, 56
   residential 11, 13
   social care 10–11, 13, 56
sharps 56, 66
signs and notices 65
6Cs 28
social care settings 10–11, 13, 56
social inclusion 50
social services 11
sonographer 45
special educational needs 18, 33
staff training see training
standardisation of care 29–30
stimulation, lack of 33
support groups 11
top exam tips 9
training
   accident prevention 67
   five Rs 54
   safeguarding 19–20, 51, 53–4
translator 44
trust 21
vegetarian diet 13
verbal communication 36–7
voice-activated software 44
vulnerable individuals 50
waste disposal 56
written exam breakdown 6

Exam-style question answers at www.hoddereducation.co.uk/myrevisionnotesdownloads